# Deciphering the Eastern Mediterranean's Hydrocarbon Dynamics

# Deciphering the Eastern Mediterranean's Hydrocarbon Dynamics: Unravelling Regional Shifts

BY

**BAHROOZ JAAFAR JABBAR**

*Mediterranean Institute for Regional Studies, Iraq*

United Kingdom – North America – Japan – India – Malaysia – China

Emerald Publishing Limited
Emerald Publishing, Floor 5, Northspring, 21-23 Wellington Street, Leeds LS1 4DL.

First edition 2024

Copyright © 2024 Bahrooz Jaafar Jabbar.
Published under exclusive licence by Emerald Publishing Limited.

**Reprints and permissions service**
Contact: www.copyright.com

No part of this book may be reproduced, stored in a retrieval system, transmitted in any form or by any means electronic, mechanical, photocopying, recording or otherwise without either the prior written permission of the publisher or a licence permitting restricted copying issued in the UK by The Copyright Licensing Agency and in the USA by The Copyright Clearance Center. Any opinions expressed in the chapters are those of the authors. Whilst Emerald makes every effort to ensure the quality and accuracy of its content, Emerald makes no representation implied or otherwise, as to the chapters' suitability and application and disclaims any warranties, express or implied, to their use.

**British Library Cataloguing in Publication Data**
A catalogue record for this book is available from the British Library

ISBN: 978-1-83608-143-2 (Print)
ISBN: 978-1-83608-142-5 (Online)
ISBN: 978-1-83608-144-9 (Epub)

INVESTOR IN PEOPLE

# Contents

| | |
|---|---|
| List of Abbreviations | *ix* |
| About the Author | *xi* |
| Preface | *xiii* |
| **Introduction** | *1* |
| **Chapter One  General Framework of the Mediterranean Geopolitics** | *5* |
| 1.1. Geopolitics: Context and Features | *5* |
| 1.2. Geopolitical Importance of the Mediterranean Sea | *8* |
| 1.2.1. The Great Powers' Desire to Control the Mediterranean Region | *9* |
| 1.2.2. Hydrocarbon as a Powder Keg in the Eastern Mediterranean | *11* |
| 1.3. Crucial Conflicts in the Eastern Mediterranean | *13* |
| 1.3.1. Syrian Crisis and the Energy Discourse | *13* |
| 1.3.2. The Turkey and Cyprus Problem in the Tinderbox of the Eastern Mediterranean | *16* |
| 1.3.3. Arab–Israeli Conflict | *24* |
| 1.3.4. Lebanon and Israel: From a Long Conflict to an Agreement | *27* |
| **Chapter Two  Oil and Natural Gas, Water Demarcation, and Electrification on the Mediterranean** | *29* |
| 2.1. International Political Economy of Oil and Gas | *29* |
| 2.2. Geopolitics of Oil | *30* |
| 2.2.1. The Implication of Uncertainty on Oil Geopolitics | *31* |
| 2.2.2. Cooperation and Competition in Oil-Producing Countries | *33* |
| 2.3. The Political Economy of Hydrocarbon in the Eastern Mediterranean | *34* |

|       |                                                                 |    |
|-------|-----------------------------------------------------------------|----|
| 2.4.  | Water Resources Among Mediterranean Countries                   | 36 |
|       | 2.4.1. Demarcation of Water: Another Wetland in the Mediterranean Region | 37 |
| 2.5.  | The Electrification of the Mediterranean Region                 | 40 |

## Chapter Three  The Regional Chessboard in the Eastern Mediterranean: A Call for Superpower    41

| 3.1.  | Israel's Mediterranean Pipedream: From Importing to Exporting Gas | 42 |
|-------|-------------------------------------------------------------------|----|
|       | 3.1.1. Israel's Import History                                    | 43 |
| 3.2.  | The Eastern Mediterranean Pipeline: Source of Tension or Regional Collaboration? | 46 |
| 3.3.  | The Egyptian Gas Market: A Gas Supplier to the European Countries | 48 |
| 3.4.  | Cyprus Gas: Position on Sovereignty and Its Market Developments   | 50 |
|       | 3.4.1. Sovereignty Versus Equality: Some Ramifications of the Cypriot Natural Gas Sector | 51 |
|       | 3.4.2. Aphrodite Gas Field: A Gift or a Curse?                    | 52 |
|       | 3.4.3. Exploration and Market Trends in the Cypriot Gas Sector    | 53 |
| 3.5.  | Egypt and Trilateral Partnerships                                 | 54 |
|       | 3.5.1. The Egyptian, Greek, and Cypriot Triangle                  | 54 |
|       | 3.5.2. Egypt–Israel Gas Export Partnership                        | 55 |
|       | 3.5.3. Egypt–Israeli Gas Supply and Purchase Agreement            | 55 |
|       | 3.5.4. Egypt and Turkey: Continued Tensions or Common Ground for Rapprochement? | 56 |
| 3.6.  | Turkey and Its Geo-Strategic Vision Toward Natural Gas in the Eastern Mediterranean and Europe | 56 |
| 3.7.  | Israeli–Europe Gas Trade                                          | 58 |
| 3.8.  | Egypt–European Gas Trade                                          | 59 |
| 3.9.  | Cypriot– European Gas Trade                                       | 59 |
| 3.10. | The Syrian Crisis within the New Geopolitical Change in the Mediterranean | 60 |
|       | 3.10.1. Syrian Oil and Gas: How Did It Influence the Syrian Crisis? | 61 |

## Chapter Four  Oil and Gas in the Iraqi Kurdistan: Geopolitical Connectivity and the Market Realities    63

| 4.1. | An Overview of the De-facto Kurdistan Region – Iraq             | 63 |
|------|-----------------------------------------------------------------|----|
| 4.2. | How Does the KRI's Hydrocarbon Secure International Support?    | 67 |

| | | |
|---|---|---|
| 4.3. | The Reality of the Crude Oil and Gas Production Industry in the Kurdistan Region; Iraq's Unstable | 68 |
| 4.4. | The KRI's Oil and Gas Blocks | 69 |
| | 4.4.1. Major Fields | 70 |
| 4.5. | Mid-Sized and Less Productive Fields | 71 |
| 4.6. | The KRI's Energy Chessboard: A Call for Realism and Superpower | 72 |
| 4.7. | Iron is Hammered When Hot: The KRI Required to Remain Sold | 75 |
| 4.8. | Can Natural Gas Become a Turning Point in the Geopolitics of the KRG? | 76 |
| 4.9. | KRG's Oil Flow to the Mediterranean: A Focus on the Future | 79 |

## Chapter Five  Intertwining of the New Global and Regional Order in the Mediterranean Region    85

| | | |
|---|---|---|
| 5.1. | Highlighting the US Agenda in the Eastern Mediterranean | 86 |
| | 5.1.1. The United States and Prospects for a New Regional Security System in the Eastern Mediterranean | 87 |
| 5.2. | Russian Foreign Policy in the Mediterranean: An Adventure or a New Paradigm? | 90 |
| | 5.2.1. Has Russia Succeeded with Its Presence in the Eastern Mediterranean? | 91 |
| 5.3. | European Union and the Eastern Mediterranean Hydrocarbon Issue | 94 |
| | 5.3.1. NATO and the Suspended Problems in the Mediterranean Basin | 95 |
| 5.4. | Intertwining International Actors in the Eastern Mediterranean | 96 |
| 5.5. | Theoretical Arguments on the Eastern Mediterranean Hydrocarbon Issue | 97 |
| | 5.5.1. Neorealist Perspective | 97 |
| | 5.5.2. Neoliberal Institutional Perspective | 99 |
| | 5.5.3. Energy Securitization in the Eastern Mediterranean: What Does the Regional Security Complex (RSC) Theory Propose? | 99 |

## Chapter Six  Environmental Crisis as a Common Ground: Is There Room for Climate Change Challenges in the Eastern Mediterranean Hydrocarbon Issue?    101

| | | |
|---|---|---|
| 6.1. | The Problems Linked to Human and Geographic Nature of the Mediterranean Region | 101 |
| | 6.1.1. Problems Related to the Relationship Between the Countries in the Mediterranean | 102 |

6.1.2. Human Security Concerns in the Mediterranean Region  104
6.1.3. How Oil and Gas Industry Affect the Climate Change in the Eastern Mediterranean?  105
6.1.4. The EU and Its Response to the Environmental Catastrophe in the Mediterranean Region  106

Conclusion  111

References  115

# List of Abbreviations

| | |
|---|---|
| **EEZ** | Exclusive Economic Zone |
| **EMGF** | Eastern Mediterranean Gas Forum |
| **EU** | European Union |
| **EMP** | Euro-Mediterranean Partnership |
| **IEA** | International Energy Agency |
| **ISIS** | Islamic State of Iraq and Syria |
| **KRG** | Kurdistan Regional Government |
| **KRI** | Kurdistan Region of Iraq |
| **LNG** | Liquefied Natural Gas |
| **NATO** | North Atlantic Treaty Organization |
| **OPEC** | Organization of the Petroleum Exporting Countries |
| **PSC** | Production Sharing Contract |
| **RoC** | Republic of Cyprus |
| **TRNC** | Turkish Republic of Northern Cyprus |
| **UFM** | Union for the Mediterranean |
| **USA** | United States of America |

# About the Author

**Bahrooz Jaafar Jabbar** hails from Iraq's Kurdistan Region. He holds a Ph.D. in International Relations from Cyprus International University, Nicosia. With over 16 years of expertise in energy geopolitics, energy security, regional order in the Middle East and Eastern Mediterranean, and ongoing conflicts in Iraq, he is the Founder and Head of the Mediterranean Institute for Regional Studies.

Dr Bahrooz has published numerous academic research papers, policy papers, and analytical articles in international scientific journals and think tanks. Most of his work can be found on www.mirs.co, available in English, Arabic, and Kurdish. Notably, his latest academic publications have garnered significant attention. The first, titled "Mediterranean Hydrocarbon Issue and Its Impact on Environmental Crisis – A Kin-State Case Dimension on Cyprus," was published in the prestigious *Sustainability* journal, boasting an impact factor of 3.889. The second publication was an academic book chapter, "Charting the Course: Geopolitical Dynamics and Market Realities in the Iraqi Kurdistan Energy Sector," which was published by "Springer," a renowned German multinational publishing company specializing in science, humanities, technical, and medical publishing.

Dr Bahrooz's insights are highly regarded by media outlets, research centers, and decision-makers, particularly regarding capacity building, energy security, non-state actors, energy geopolitics, and political economy in the Eastern Mediterranean and Middle East. He is recognized as an Iraqi Kurdish academician and completed a six-month teaching methods course at Charmo University, earning a pedagogical certificate internationally recognized by the Ministry of Higher Education of the Kurdistan Regional Government.

You can follow Dr Bahrooz Jaafar on X- Twitter (@bahroozJaafar) and LinkedIn (BahroozJaafar) or contact him via email at Jafarbahroz@gmail.com

# Preface

This book aims to analyze the political economy of hydrocarbons in the Eastern Mediterranean and the factors influencing their energy development. It effectively argues that the region's geopolitical landscape, particularly concerning hydrocarbons, is intricately linked to political, economic, and environmental considerations. The central argument emphasizes the significance of the region's energy dynamics and the roles of key players. To support these arguments, the book meticulously presents a comprehensive array of evidence, including historical context, geopolitical shifts, economic data, and the involvement of major powers. The integration of statistics and agreements, along with the establishment of the Eastern Mediterranean Gas Forum, serves to fortify the evidential foundation. To this effect, the book focuses on the critical challenges in the Eastern Mediterranean within the emerging regional order and aims to investigate the role played by extra-regional actors such as NATO, Russia, and the United States. The Mediterranean basin holds significant geostrategic importance, serving as a meeting point between Asia, Europe, and Africa. Its status reflects the intensity of commercial and military traffic, making it the southern base of NATO and Russia's primary gateway to warm waters. Additionally, the trilateral alliance between Greece, Cyprus, and Israel has been embraced by the United States, with hopes that offshore energy production in the Eastern Mediterranean will establish a new security framework and impact global energy markets.

# Introduction

The Mediterranean Sea has many key roles in different aspects: Geographically, it is a point of entrance and a bridge between the Middle East, Europe, and North Africa. Historically, it has been the cradle of civilization; then it played an extremely significant role when it came to the affairs of empires such as the Roman Empire, the Ottoman Empire, and the Great Britain. Nowadays, superpowers such as the United States, Russia, China, and NATO have various projects and initiatives in this area. Economically, the main issue is the discovery and export of natural gas and oil since the end of 2010; in addition to the issues of shipping and oil transportation through the Mediterranean Sea, water delineation, and the issue of renewable energy and electrification (Dalay, 2021).

All of these crucial roles of the Mediterranean basin have made it a matter of security and stability not only for the Eastern Mediterranean or the Middle East but for the entire world. New conflicts and various threats can also arise in the region, as the world's most sensitive issues involve the Mediterranean, such as the emergence of immigration and crossing hundreds of thousands of refugees from the Middle East and North Africa to Europe, the Palestinian–Israeli conflict, the Syrian crisis, and regional incursion, the unsolved problem of Cyprus between Turkey and the European Union on one side, between Turkey and Republic of Cyprus on the other side. Additionally, the collapsing balance of power ties between the countries in the Eastern Mediterranean: Egypt–Turkey, Turkey–Israel, Turkey–Greece, Turkey–Cyprus, Turkey–Syria, and the tensions between the EU and Turkey. This has had economic, humanitarian, regional, and international conflicts since the Arab spring's uprising (2011).

The hydrocarbon landscape in the Eastern Mediterranean is intricately woven with political and economic considerations, demanding a nuanced exploration of various facets. A comprehensive analysis must delve into the complex interplay of factors influencing energy development in the region. This encompasses understanding the political economy governing hydrocarbons, elucidating the strategic importance of the Eastern Mediterranean, and delineating its role within the broader global energy markets.

Central to this exploration are the key regional players and alliances that shape the trajectory of energy dynamics. Israel, Egypt, and Cyprus emerge as pivotal actors, necessitating a thorough re-evaluation of their roles in this geopolitical landscape. Each nation's stance on hydrocarbon utilization and exploration profoundly impacts the region's overall energy strategy.

---

Deciphering the Eastern Mediterranean's Hydrocarbon Dynamics:
Unravelling Regional Shifts, 1–4
Copyright © 2024 by Bahrooz Jaafar Jabbar
Published under exclusive licence by Emerald Publishing Limited
doi:10.1108/978-1-83608-142-520241001

Moreover, the geopolitical and security dimensions of the Eastern Mediterranean must be considered. A detailed examination is imperative to unravel the alliances and conflicts that define the region's geopolitical landscape. Simultaneously, considerations of security are paramount, not only for the nations directly involved but also for global energy markets that are significantly influenced by developments in this strategic area.

Environmental hazards add another layer of complexity to the narrative. The exploration and exploitation of hydrocarbons inevitably pose risks to the delicate ecological balance of the Eastern Mediterranean. A holistic perspective must weigh the environmental consequences and advocate for sustainable practices in pursuing energy resources.

In this context, the trilateral alliance between Greece, Cyprus, and Israel assumes significance. The US endorsement of this alliance signals a recognition of its potential to reshape the region's security framework. The hope is that offshore energy production in the Eastern Mediterranean will enhance regional security and exert a transformative influence on global energy markets.

In general, a comprehensive examination of the Eastern Mediterranean's political economy of hydrocarbons necessitates a multidimensional approach. Understanding the strategic, geopolitical, security, and environmental dimensions is crucial for charting a sustainable and secure energy future in the region. The trilateral alliance, backed by the United States, emerges as a pivotal force that could steer the Eastern Mediterranean toward a new era of energy stability and global impact.

Events are occurring so dramatically and rapidly in the first quarter of the 21$^{st}$ century that scientists and international relations literature may need help to name and define developments. Here are more than 10 years (from 2010 to 2023) of discovering and extracting natural gas from Israel's waterfront and Cyprus that led to media and research centers investigating. This has encouraged the energy enterprises to move toward the area under the direct supervision of the US administration. And then the Eastern Mediterranean Gas Forum (EMGF) has established in September 2020 between Egypt, the Republic of Cyprus, Israel, Greece, Jordan, Palestine Authority, France, and Italy. Each of the energy ministers of Greece, Israel Cyprus signed the final agreement for the pipeline project in January 2020 to transport Cyprus and Israeli gas to Greece, Italy, and other European countries.

In fact, building a 1,900 km of underwater pipelines at a cost of about $7 billion in such a sensitive geographical area is a meaningful project. Since 2010, it has been viewed that the East-Med gas project becomes an alternative to Russian natural gas to Europe or at least reduce Europe's dependence on Russian energy. Also, the event has turned Israel from an importer of natural gas to an energy exporter! Furthermore, these changes encouraged other regional powers and countries to move the region. For instance, the UAE, although not geographically linked to the Eastern Mediterranean, has joined as a member of the EMGF and Israel has sold a 22% stake in the Tamar gas field to the UAE's Mubadala Petroleum for 1.2$billion (Anadolu Agency, 2021).

In the most straightforward vision, oil and natural gas are still the world's first commercial commodities. Billions of cars, planes, ships, factories, electricity networks, and various manufacturing industries still wholly depend on oil and gas. Without natural gas and oil, moving and transportation will stop. Even though humanity has reached high levels of development and is a marvelous invention in its history, it is yet to be able to replace oil and natural gas. As stone coal had a significant influence in the previous centuries, its role changed to oil, and now natural gas is at the height of its life. Natural gas has never affected international relations as much as it did in 2022 and 2023.

Hence, the political economy of hydrocarbons is related to two key concepts: The first is energy geopolitics, which is the result of the effects of geographical and political factors on the existence of oil and natural gas. This has a direct reflection on the way countries are dealing with their outside borders. The second is energy security, which means connection and balance between national security and sufficient embodiment of economical natural resources for using and filling local needs.

According to the US Energy Information Administration, in 1980, the world used 53 trillion cubic feet of natural gas, but in 2010, 113 trillion cubic feet of natural gas were used in the world (U.S. Energy Information Administration, 2012). As pointed out by the International Energy Agency, in 2023, global gas demand rose by just 0.5%, as growth in China, North America, and gas-rich countries in Africa and the Middle East was partially offset by declines in other regions. In 2024, global gas demand is forecast to grow by 2.5% and rise to 4.19 trillion cubic meters (International Energy Agency, 2023). In regards to oil, similarly, in 2023, it amounted to 102.21 million barrels daily. The source expects the oil demand to increase to 104 million barrels per day by the end of 2024 (Statista, 2024). The demand for natural gas and oil has increased further.

The primary goal of this book can be encapsulated in the following query:

*Are the geopolitical changes in the Eastern Mediterranean directly related to the issue of natural gas and oil; or are there some other backgrounds to these changes?*

To address this question head-on it is imperative to pose two additional questions: What is the role of the superpowers in determining and settling the regional conflicts in the Eastern Mediterranean? Has the extraction and export of natural gas in the Eastern Mediterranean encouraged regional conflicts; or has it become a reason for new regional cooperation and calling for the surrounding countries to find a new common regional security system?

To this effect, this book can be viewed as a rich scientific source from various angles, such as:

- It helps us to better understand the importance of Eastern Mediterranean geopolitics and identify the crucial conflicts in the region.
- It offers in-depth knowledge on the political economy of oil and natural gas in general, and on the actions of the multi-national corporations specifically in the Eastern Mediterranean.

- The book also seeks to explain the regional chessboard in the Eastern Mediterranean and each player's role in it; like Israel, Egypt, Cyprus, Turkey, and Greece, as well as the illustrations with the realist approach within the international relations literature.
- It interprets the intersection of the new global and regional order in the Eastern Mediterranean.
- The work highlights the division of the reality of power due to the sensitive issues in the region, such as hydrocarbon capacities, electrifications, water demarcation, environmental problems, and regional security challenges, while more importantly, it focuses on strengthening the Eastern Mediterranean bloc by controlling and patrolling other nearby oil and natural gas-rich regions like the Kurdistan Region of Iraq.

Chapter One

# General Framework of the Mediterranean Geopolitics

## Abstract

The geopolitical significance of the Mediterranean Sea transcends regional security and energy supply, profoundly impacting global security dynamics. Daily headlines underscore the plight of migrants from the Middle East and North Africa crossing the Mediterranean, exacerbating humanitarian crises and European identity challenges. Environmental concerns are further heightened by the abundance of global ports facilitating oil and goods transportation, alongside the staggering number of tourists flocking to the Mediterranean coast annually. This chapter serves as a gateway to the book, exploring the concept of "geopolitics" and delineating its characteristics. It specifically delves into the political economy of the Eastern Mediterranean and the geopolitical obstacles to energy security in the region. The chapter strategically selects four primary issues to dissect the region's conflict complexity: the Syrian crisis, the Israeli–Palestinian conflict, the unresolved Cyprus dispute, and the Lebanon–Israel conflict over water border demarcation.

*Keywords*: Geopolitics; Mediterranean Sea; conflict dynamics; energy security; exclusive economic zone (EEZ)

## 1.1. Geopolitics: Context and Features

Every concept has a history and geography; "geopolitics" is no exception. As Tuathail (1998) pointed out, the term "geopolitics" was first used in 1899 by Swedish political scientist Rudolf Kjellén. The 20th century is widely regarded as the century of geopolitics. From the term's inception at the start of the century to its widespread usage today as an indicator of global strife and change, the geopolitical dilemma provides an insightful window into the major power and space contests that have dominated this era. It has significantly evolved from Kjellén's original definition in his research to denote a broad interest in the intersection of geography and politics. Defining geopolitics precisely is challenging because the meaning of terms like these tends to shift with different historical eras and world-order systems.

Geopolitics is best understood in its historical and discursive context of use. In the early 20th century, Kjellen and other imperialist thinkers understood geopolitics as that part of Western imperial knowledge that dealt with the relationship between the physical earth and politics. Associated later with the notorious Nazi foreign policy goal of Lebensraum (the pursuit of more "living space" for the German nation), the term fell out of favor with many writers and commentators after World War II (Tuathail, 1998).

The fundamentals of geopolitics form with the unique imperatives and constraints of nation-states. They involve looking at all the attributes that affect a country or a region, dissecting each piece to better comprehend its implications, then putting them back together and painting a picture clear enough for others to understand. However, a good starting place is comprehending the elements that make up the fundamentals of geopolitics, how they interact and how they affect the whole of a country. These elements concern geography, politics, economics, military, technology, and culture. Each element is important to the country's geopolitical "picture" certainly.

The foremost factor is "Geography," which affects every element of a country's geopolitical context. Heartly, the geography of a place defines it. It determines what economic sectors will grow. It can influence how centralized power may be and a country's susceptibility to invasion or need for alliances. For example, nation-states like Russia may expand their borders to defend their political center. The larger this buffer zone is, the more secure Russia is from invading European powers. This fear of invasion is a big part of Russia's obsession with Ukraine. The closer Ukraine draws to Europe for its security, trade, and political alliance, the more threatened Russia will feel.

Geography also affects the military conditions of a country. Long coastal zones often need a navy; terrain dictates the equipment and skill set required for an army, and a country's general expansiveness defines the size and needs for an air force. As well as, the military can protect a country's borders, project power overseas, and defend against threats. A powerful military can significantly influence a country's geopolitical power projection and impact its interaction with neighboring countries. Countries under direct threat of foreign military forces must find ways to secure their defense and interests, such as through international alliances or enhancing their military to balance the power dynamics (Geopolitical Futures, 2022).

Another constituent element is "Politics," which can be defined simply as how a country is governed. The political dynamic of a country directly affects its institutional effectiveness, social stability, and international engagement strategy. While we at Geopolitical Futures do not predict a nation's domestic election outcomes, the changes in political systems can impact other arenas of geopolitics, such as military and economics. Rather than the decisions made by a single leader, however, we look at politics from the perspective of imperatives versus constraints. This basic dynamic forms the foundation of our analytical strategy, and has proved to be an excellent characteristic to define and determine how a government may act next. This means that we can generally determine how a nation-state will behave/act and what it will prioritize, no matter who is in charge of it (Tuathail, 1998).

Economic is another feature of Geopolitics; the economy of a country or a region plays a significant role in determining its overall stability and power. A vigorous economy is often necessary for a powerful military and social stability. A country's economic stability, versatility, and resource availability directly impact its geopolitical behavior. For instance, countries with excess oil and gas reserves but a deficit of arable land may use economic ties with other countries to secure food and supplies for their populace in exchange for oil and natural gas. Interactions like this allow countries to use their strengths to circumvent constraints and better meet their imperatives. By this, "Geopolitical Economy" determines the significance and nature of free trade agreements (FTA).

Moreover, the technological capabilities of a country or region can also gain great economic, military, cultural, commercial, and diplomatic power. A country with modern technological capabilities can better influence the world stage (Geopolitical Futures, 2022).

Furthermore, there is a direct relationship between geopolitics and culture. Geopolitics describes and denotes how diverse groups of people interact and how nation-states at large will interact with each other. As Al-Rodhan (2014) pointed out, culture has a salient geopolitical relevance in a world that defines itself by much more than diplomatic exchanges and inter-state relations. This is primarily because of identity issues' deeply visceral and emotional connotations. This has been the case throughout history, as exchanges have occurred between people of different cultures for millennia, but today, they are marked by unprecedented assertiveness and scope of relations. This presents great opportunities on several levels but also has the potential to initiate tension or conflict when combined with injustice, inequalities, and insecurities (Al-Rodhan, 2014).

Thus, geopolitics has gained much more meaning and consequences. During the later years of the Cold War, geopolitics was used to describe the global contest between the Soviet Union and the United States for influence and control over the states and strategic resources of the world. Former US Secretary of State Henry Kissinger almost single-handedly helped to revive the term in the 1970s by using it as a synonym for the superpower game of balance-of-power politics played out across the global political map (Tuathail, 1998).

Since then, geopolitics has enjoyed a revival of interest worldwide as foreign policymakers, strategic analysts, transnational managers, and academics have struggled to make sense of the dynamics of the world political map. Geopolitics has become popular again because it deals with comprehensive visions of the world political map. Geopolitics addresses the "big picture" and offers a way of relating local and regional dynamics to the global system.

## 1.2. Geopolitical Importance of the Mediterranean Sea

Mediterranean is a region of shared problems and shared opportunities within contested domination control leading to the redistribution of power and determination of the future of the region. Models of studying the Mediterranean have presented it as a region of effervesce political developments which may have a significant world impact as a result of the entanglement of all the major global and regional powers in preserving prudential interest on the Mediterranean (Gillespie, 2013).

More specifically, the Mediterranean is a linking point of Europe, North Africa, and the Middle East countries with the United States stretching its influence to the region through allies and proxies. Countries in Europe's political circumference, especially Italy and Greece, have the hinge of their borders on the Mediterranean Sea. Historically, the Mediterranean Sea has been a source of security or insecurity but certainly a source of prosperity to these countries. Events like the refugee crisis in Libya and other countries in North Africa, and Syria in the Middle East have also been impacted by the connection to the sea. Scholars have presented the region as the determinant of which power controls Eurasia (Holland, 2015).

In 1980, gas was first discovered in the Mediterranean region across the Egyptian sea and within the Nile delta toward northern Alexandria (Dolson et al., 2000). This has led several countries in the Mediterranean and outside the region to begin to examine the possibility of oil and gas on their offshore. Consequently, there have been changes in the form of legislation that pertains to the discovery of oil and who owns a particular offshore, when should the offshore be established, how should the oil be drilled, what channel should the pipe run through and who should partake in the profit that is derived from oil and gas.

The international oil companies have engaged in huge investments in reaching out to the Mediterranean countries to be able to take advantage of the drilling opportunities by signing contracts and deals that give them the right to offshore drilling. They have been caught as the political tension, contest, and context of the region erupted much more after the discovery of oil and gas. Despite this challenge, the companies have found alternatives whenever they encounter the political-economic context of the Mediterranean hydrocarbon. These companies were able to use their heavy petrochemical plants established in less contested parts of the Mediterranean to supply gas, especially in Cairo to power the residential environment.

Although there has been a massive discovery of gas on the Mediterranean, statistics has signaled that it might not be enough for the consumption of countries in the region and their desired level of export. It is only a reserve of about 35 trillion cubic feet; hence a contest is inevitable as well as a search for new reserves. Every oil and gas company did not mind the contest as they engage bilaterally with each individual country in the region to explore their waters for more discoveries. The paradox is that the more the discoveries, the more complicated the politics, economy, and energy discourse of the Mediterranean. As the countries engaged in claims to the hydrocarbon by measuring offshore rights and fields, their internal politics also changed to adapt to the contest and the consumption of the Mediterranean oil and gas (Alsharhan, 2003).

### 1.2.1. The Great Powers' Desire to Control the Mediterranean Region

The superpowers have at different points benefited from the strategic importance of the Mediterranean Sea as a point of passage to access other parts of the world in continuation of their influence. Great Britain had registered its interest in the region and aimed to maintain its presence for its strategic purposes such as overlapping political and economic domination. Controlling the Mediterranean for the Great Britain was a direct action manifesting its naval superiority across the Mediterranean until the 19th century (Gaiser & Hribar, 2012).

Compared to the British Empire's domination and the 8th-century domination by the Roman Empire, no other power has been able to use the Mediterranean as a direct access point to its control of the world. Italian republics and their maritime have made attempts, however, they have only controlled some parts of the Mediterranean through their potentates. As the dynamics of global politics changed over time that controlling the sea as an empire like Great Britain became unacceptable to the international community considering the geopolitical distance of Great Britain (Roucek, 1953).

Hence, the United States move to control the sea has been through the creation of allies in the region. Alongside its allies, the United States makes geopolitical decisions and actions that would promote its interest in the region since controlling the sea is having access to the three significant geopolitical zones. It has, through this halted the domination of other powers (Camprubí, 2020). Entering into European political dynamics suffices as a cogent reason for countries to seek the control of the sea. European political climate, more specifically the European Union has been led by France and Germany whose rivalry in the region has also included attempts of domination or at least controlling the countries that hinge on the Mediterranean Sea whether ran Africa or the Middle East.

The great powers' desire to control the Mediterranean region has historical, geopolitical, economic, and military roots. As the Sixth Fleet moved into the Mediterranean shortly after the Second World War in 1950, US hegemony in this Sea was barely contested. The US Navy's dominance in southern Europe was still unrivaled twenty years later, but the situation underwater was quite different. Between the nationalization and initial closure of the Suez Canal in 1956 and the Arab–Israeli war in 1973, the Eastern Mediterranean experienced what must have been the largest buildup of US and Russian submarines per cubic meter in history (Camprubí, 2020).

The Mediterranean Sea connects three strategic regions: Southern Europe, North Africa, and the Middle East, so US foreign policy to control or influence the Mediterranean has become a policy of control or influence over these three regions. For North Africa, some proponents of democracy have argued that the US desires to impose democracy in the region considering democracy and peace as the need of North Africa. More considerably, it is more near to accurate to argue that the US seeks to establish a friendly line of countries on the shore, democratic or non-democratic. These would include countries that could share and promote American policies toward Africa (Woodward, 2016).

For the Middle East, security studies scholars have argued that the US would seek to create a stable Middle East to bring about peace and a more progressive friendliness among the countries in the region. Such arguments ignore the more closely knitted American–Israeli relations compared to the relations with other countries in the region. Hence, the US possession of Mediterranean control toward the Middle East is to promote the recognition of Israel's statehood or the normalization of relations with Israel by the Arab countries. Achieving this would mean creating a more stable interaction in the region, however on the account of normalization of the Arab–Israeli relations (Prifti, 2017). In Europe, the United States would maintain a close ally's interest in security and prosperity in its influence on the sea in congruence with the goals of the long-established integration that is ongoing in the European Union (Cox & Stokes, 2018).

The Mediterranean has also been a lever of influence over these regions. A point of clash between the European powers such as Britain, France, and Germany, in addition to America's influence, it has attracted the attention of Russia and China to the ongoing clash in the region, therefore making them create allies that provide their interests in the region (Shaffer, 2018). Russia's influence in the region has been through its long-standing ally, Syria. The war in Syria has granted a justification for Russia to establish its presence in the Mediterranean through Russian forces that have been present in Syria. Irrespective of how small or indirect Russia's influence is, it has given it another position within European politics through its presence in Syria, hence a niche in the Mediterranean.

China likewise has also registered its possible influence on the seas as it strategically invests in the Southeastern Europe through its Belt Road as well as its acquisition strategy that granted it the opportunity to take over properties of other countries like railroads and airports for an extended period of time. This grants China the opportunity to influence the politics of all countries where its investments and acquisitions are present. This discourse shows that although such outcomes for the control of the region may be perceived as a factor external to the actors and to the Mediterranean Sea itself, however to assume that the only importance of the Mediterranean in for passage and control of the region will be to limit the significance of the seas itself (Ekman, 2018).

Hence, apart from ports and access points that Mediterranean provides, the resources in the region and the markets that it provides as countries borders around the shore are paramount in the significance of the region. The Mediterranean is a significant hub of the global economy where millions of tons of crude oil as well as natural gas have been exported from the Middle East to America and the European countries through the Suez channel. This economic and financial perspective is common among all actors that are directly or indirectly connected to the Mediterranean Sea (Rosenthal, 2013).

### 1.2.2. Hydrocarbon as a Powder Keg in the Eastern Mediterranean

The economic importance of the Mediterranean Sea advanced from being a trade route to being the source of the product that is being traded. Oil and other products have been traded along the Mediterranean Sea which has been the essence of control of the Mediterranean Sea (Özgür, 2017). However, the discovery of the existing offshore hydrocarbon has made the region of greater significance than in previous decades. This new importance has sparked new assertions on the control of the region as countries on the Mediterranean claim delimitation of their maritime zones as a result of the competition for the rights to make use of the rich energy resources in their national interests and in the favor of allies or members of alliance or international organizations such as the European Union.

This involves exerting more political influence on the region more than in the previous centuries and decades. The United States Geological Survey measured that the region has about 1.7 billion barrels of oil and possesses the possibility of about 2 trillion-meter square of natural gas. This has been estimated to be able to meet the regions' demand for oil and natural gas, thereby replacing suppliers such as Russia, not only in the region but also providing alternatives to the European Union, Turkey, and all other long dependent on the Russia's oil. The region itself would be able to benefit from this oil for three decades as well as exporting the oil to other parts of the world (Feng & Reshef, 2016).

The discovery of hydrocarbon places the region on a prosperity path; however, it aggravates the salient problem of political control in the region. The blessing of hydrocarbon can therefore become a curse as a result of the contestation which is taking place to claim access and make use of the resources rather than being a means to resolving the struggle for power that has existed in the region. The volatility of the energy prices has become the pressure on which most of the countries are insistently pursuing the control of the region's hydrocarbon in order to be on a safe haven if they can significantly get a good share of the oil. Consequently, tensions have risen as the control of hydrocarbon exacerbates the already politically tense situation in the region rather than abate the struggle among littoral countries. The current question is to what extent have these discoveries affected the fabric of the Mediterranean and its already existing Mediterranean problem. Hence, the further question of how international order or more specifically regional order can bring about a co-habitable Mediterranean where political and economic contestation can be resolved without an escalation or curbing of the ongoing confrontations among stakeholders in the region (Grigoriadis, 2014).

To limit the region to the action or influence of one great power ignores the constellation of problems and challenges that are on the Mediterranean. Hence, the hydrocarbon discovery has been discussed. It is therefore important to understand the Mediterranean's overlapping dynamics with regards to the configuration of countries as allies or foes in taking advantage of the hydrocarbon and other resources of the Mediterranean.

Considering the contestation for the control of the region and the decision of what the geopolitical state will become, several actors have been using links and leverages to reposition themselves in the region. The United States has the presence of its ally, Israel in the region and has been a major player in the region since the mid-20th century (Inbar, 2014).

The European Union penetrates the region through the presence of its members, Greece and since 2003 Cyprus to claim influence in the region. France as a major actor in the European Union has also individually allied in-line with the interests of Greece and Cyprus to control the opportunities in the region while determining the direction of the solutions to the problems that are in the region (Gillespie, 2011).

Turkey on one side has sought to also influence its power in the region by focusing on its central geopolitical position, specifically being the country in the central position where the West and the Middle East meet. More significantly, the presence of its kin state in the Northern Cyprus has been the current and ongoing medium by which it tries to take advantage of the opportunities on the Mediterranean, which clashes with Greece's and Cyprus' pursuit on the Mediterranean as a result of the Cyprus conflict (Ulusoy, 2020).

> European nations are endeavoring to reduce their reliance on Russia for energy matters. This creates a noteworthy opportunity for Turkey to establish itself as a key player in facilitating the linkage of alternative energy sources to Europe.

Furthermore, the Middle East's, especially the Gulf countries' relations with Turkey have been characterized by conflict in the regional governance of the Middle East. This has created an anti-Turkey front in the Middle East, which was evident in the UAE's competitive attitude as a result of the strained relations between the other Middle East countries (Gürel & Cornu, 2013).

However, between 2021 and 2022, Turkey normalized relations with two important Middle Eastern states, the UAE and Israel. Then, Turkey's foreign policy desired to show a new Turkey under President Erdoğan, which would change its address and style. Nevertheless, the region's countries must see this intention under Erdoğan's presidency. Because at the same time, Turkey repeatedly threatened countries in the region, including Greece, in 2022 when Turkey's president Recep Tayyip Erdoğan expressed, "*Suddenly come,*" "*Suddenly come down,*" and "*We may suddenly arrive one night*" (Haartz, 2022).

The Mediterranean features constellations of challenges which include the Arab Spring involving Tunisia, Libya, and Syria as the Mediterranean countries that experienced the Arab Spring. The countries' experience of internal instability has affected their position in the Mediterranean as they had to focus more on resolving the internal problem than stretching forth to take a share of the hydrocarbon on the sea. Libya for example lacks a coordinated government that can chart its foreign policy regarding the Mediterranean and the countries seeking control of the region.

The NATO intervention in Libya could be argued as also a means to gain access in the region for its resources. No country has been able to exploit the issue to enter into the Mediterranean; however, Syria has helped its long-standing ally,

Russia throws unreserved support toward Damascus. The Syrian state of internal instability has been part of the Arab Spring, however, unlike Libya that has resulted in a failed state, the Syrian government under Bashir Assad has continued to lead the country with Russia's support. Hence, its stake in the Mediterranean can be defined by its government and the influence of Moscow on its foreign policy. Unlike Libya and Syria, the Arab Spring in Tunisia has led to the change of government which has in many ways seemed to be the goal of the uprising and therefore it has not escalated in the manner of a lingering crisis as observed in Libya and Syria (Bauer, 2013).

Therefore, the Mediterranean is significant from a political-economic standpoint as countries seek to gain political control to determine the direction of order in the region as well as take advantage of the hydrocarbon discovery in favor of their national interests. This is wrapped in already existing conflicts and the creation of new crucial conflicts in the region. These dynamics of the Mediterranean are expected to transcend into a new regional order.

Among all the contestations that are taking place in the Mediterranean, four major conflicts have been identified as the overarching challenges in the region using the following factors: *duration, complexity, positions, and role of various actors*. Lingering conflicts pinpoint the difficulty in solving the incompatibilities among parties and therefore can be used as a barometer to determine and select conflicts that are crucial in the Mediterranean.

Moreover, the duration of conflict signals the level of complexity which may be observable in such crisis. Complexity in conflict shows the number of parties and the possible solution that has been tried in an attempt to resolve the conflict. It also involves overlapping issues and countries, politics and economy as well as alliance and estranged relations. Lastly, the third yardstick is selecting crucial conflicts on the Mediterranean in the position of a country that has no defined alliance hence therefore maintains fragile relations with countries around its perimeters.

## 1.3. Crucial Conflicts in the Eastern Mediterranean

The Arab–Israeli conflict, the Syrian crisis, Turkey's position on the Mediterranean and the Cyprus conflict, and the Israeli–Lebanon border conflict have been selected to analyze the complexity of the conflict in the region.

### *1.3.1. Syrian Crisis and the Energy Discourse*

The Syrian issue is one that is locked among actors that have already been entangled in the Mediterranean issue which are Syria itself, Turkey, and the European Union. This is because the Syrian issue has become the challenge that affects all actors in a similar dimension; hence they need each other with respect to these dimensions. The concern patterning to the problems that have risen because of the Syria issue has brought Turkey and the European Union to a point of either cooperation or conflict while the energy issue of the Mediterranean remains within the discourse.

Turkey being a neighbor of Syria through border sharing has a significant interest in Syria and has been creating its involvement through since the beginning of the crisis. Such as included the criticism against the Assad's government when engaging with its citizens using force as the whirlwind of Arab spring, which pushes for changes in the government conduct toward the wellbeing of its citizens or democratization as presented by the United States and its allies hit Syria. Turkey's stance in regard to the events in Syria was to bring about the change of the regime highlighting its support for the opposition to the government (Kukushkin, 2021).

The government of Turkey has expressed this through its withdrawal of all its ties with the Assad regime and targeted its foreign policy toward Syria as a regime change policy as it condemns and accuses Assad on violating the human rights of Syrians. Since the conflict began, the Turkish government has also created opportunities for Syrians to gain status in Turkey to make them escape from the Assad government which shows Turkey's commitment to supporting the citizens of the countries in the region. It has created financial support also for Syrians. Today the streets of Turkey are filled with Syrians who benefit from the government of Turkey (Özden, 2013).

Such judgment, criticism, and positioning serve as a signal of Turkey's interest in becoming the regional power in the Middle East. Similarly, the European Union (EU) has taken the same path by enforcing sanctions and other pressuring measures on the Syrian government. The EU's promotion of democracy, and its human rights values as well as the freedom of speech and movement have been values that direct its conduct toward neighbors like Syria. Additionally, the growth of insecurity in its neighborhood has caused the EU to continue to pressure Syria to submit to democratic changes (Bilgic & Pace, 2017).

Nevertheless, there are many contentions between the two actors in regard to the Syria issue. The EU and Turkey engage from different directions on the terrorist challenges that have caused the Mediterranean region to become insecure and unstable due to regular attacks and bombings. Another issue is the Syrian refugee crisis which has led to the influx of refugees into Europe. Although these cases are expected to bring about cooperation between the EU and Turkey, the approaches of the two actors have been different, hence creating contention between them (Holtug, 2016).

The EU has sought the support of Turkey with regards to the battle against the terrorists intending to move toward Europe to cause an attack in the region as a means of jeopardizing the hope of the refugees that are seeking to move into Europe because of the war in Syria. While Turkey provides support for the opposition to be able to challenge the government and bring about change not minding the radical forces that might be part of the opposition. As a result, Turkey has placed the refugee crisis on the list of its bargaining leverages when at negotiations pertaining to the Mediterranean with the EU. This is the EU's approach, which requires Turkey to cooperate with the challenges of migrant crossings, terrorism, and any other phenomenon threatening Europe. At the same time, Turkey is a member of NATO, responsible for defending Europe's entity as a common union. Hence, positioning Turkey in a role that is significant in the Mediterranean (Betts & Collier, 2015).

The EU's goal is to ensure that ISIS and any other terrorist group do not have access to Europe and should be curbed in Syria. On the other hand, Turkey which the EU is pushing to handle the issue of terrorism on its behalf as an actor in a strategic location has been favored by Sunni Islam in its goal of establishing an opposition against the Kurdish groups and the Free Syrian Army that have a significant link with the Kurdish movement (PKK) in Turkey. Such gains on the side of Turkey have therefore become a threat to the EU's goal of using Turkey as the actor that pushes for its anti-terrorism campaign in the Mediterranean, since while the EU focuses on a general war against terrorism, Turkey is concerned about the PKK as a *"terrorist"* group and their affiliations in the region (Dal, 2016).

The EU's expectation is that Turkey will be able to cooperatively intercept every terrorist movement into Europe since it serves as a transit country between Europe and the Middle East while having its border on the Mediterranean. Rating the performance of this role of Turkey as a point of disrupting the terrorist transit to Europe, the EU has claimed that it has not sufficiently played these roles given the attacks which have taken place where the terrorists were previously seen passing through Turkey's borders. Turkey has also criticized the EU's lapses in not vetting the movement or the return of European educated Arabs to Syria to join ISIL or another terrorist group. These have been conveyed in the message of European political leaders that claimed that there is a high traffic of jihadists through Turkey. Reports, even the boats rescued with hundreds of people in the Mediterranean, show that the extremists who have arrived in Europe, Britain, come from the southern borders of the Mediterranean, thus contributing to regional and global instability (Fisseha, 2017).

Furthermore, intelligence sharing has also been a subject that has challenged the cooperation between the EU and Turkey on the terrorism and refugee issues in the Mediterranean. Turkey accused the EU of not making available the intelligence information that would support Turkey to play this role. The heights of the challenges are that the information regarding how long the individuals have stayed in the war zone, the level of radicalization that has taken place during their stay in the region, their intentions, and actions to return to Europe to carry out. This makes the sharing of intelligence, policing, and judiciary decisions very crucial in the relationship between the EU and Turkey (Fisseha, 2017).

The refugee crisis which has been caused by the Syrian civil war is the second case that is being dealt with by the EU and Turkey and it has a background that links their solutions together seeking a level of cooperation. Since the beginning of the Syrian war in 2011, millions of the population of the country fled the crisis zone to seek protection in the neighboring countries. A total of about 6 million refugees fled from Syria and sought refuge in the countries of Mediterranean. This is because the other Middle Eastern countries were also experiencing crisis and unstable; hence the southern and northern Mediterranean countries have become the destination for these refugees (Khadduri, 2012).

The EU-Mediterranean relations however have been to ensure there is a safe zone along all its borders with neighboring countries which is expressed in its neighborhood policy. More than any country in the Mediterranean, Turkey has become the host country with the highest number of refugees, as over 10,000 refugees have relocated across the Aegean Sea to reach Europe to seek asylum since the crisis began in 2011. This has resulted in a large number of asylum applications in Europe wherein the host countries are finding it very difficult to address, as the influx was exceeding the available facilities and space of the European Union, especially in terms of political and administrative procedures.

This was reflected in the crisis that occurred among the European Union members when some countries opened their borders while others closed them to the refugees, creating a decentralized response among the European Union members. Hence, the Syrian refugee crisis affected the political fabric of the supranational structure of the union as well as the value held by the members as being human rights and freedom-focused (Stocker, 2012).

Hence, the significant role of Turkey in the European Union surfaces in the refugee crisis. Being confronted with the immediate demand to control the influx of refugees through the Aegean Sea, the EU was left with no option but to approach Turkey to cooperate in a manner that curbs the migration of refugees. Firstly, the EU has presented a readmission plan for refugees to the EU which was replaced by the collection action plan of both actors where Turkey will address the human trafficking, refugee crisis, and the uncurbed migration more effectively, and in cooperation with Greece while the EU provides all the financial cost.

Meanwhile, regarding the Cyprus conflict, this is where the EU with its members Greece and Cyprus is contending with Turkey; not by the ineffectiveness of its role, but by questioning the entirety of its role and stance on the Cyprus issues (Nas, 2019 – The EU Approach to Syrian Crisis, Turkey as a Partner). There are clearly different objectives among these actors on the Cyprus nevertheless. The resourcefulness of the Mediterranean increased their desire to achieve their goals in holding on to their access in Cyprus whether the EU and Greece through its member Cyprus or whether Turkey by its presence in Northern Cyprus.

### 1.3.2. The Turkey and Cyprus Problem in the Tinderbox of the Eastern Mediterranean

Although Turkey and Greece have had a series of conflicts around the seas and claims to the islands, the issue of Cyprus has been the main problem challenging the two countries' relations since the coup d'état in Cyprus and the intervention of Turkey in 1974. The growing contention between Turkey and Greece has created difficulty in handling the Cyprus problem. There have been arguments that the issue should be left to the Greek and Turkish Cypriots to resolve; however, Greece and Turkey have influenced decisions and negotiation plans brought by the two primary parties, the Greek and Turkish Cypriots. Both countries' foreign policies toward each other have included the Cyprus clause.

This is because they have maintained a level of national commitment to the Cypriots on both the Greek and Turkish sides since the Ottomans' rule. Hence, the presence of Greece and Turkey in Cyprus shows that they intend to hold on to their security interests in the country, since they have had a historical enmity since the Ottoman period. Hence, losing Cyprus to Greece on the side of Turkey is a great threat to its vital interests. Consequently, the issue remains unresolved, and the island is divided between the two sides (as depicted in Fig. 1). Also, all the other islands will be easily yielded to Turkey if Cyprus, the biggest among them, is granted to Greece. All these arguments are the rationale behind the Turkish intervention in Cyprus as the coup took place (Fouskas, 2001; Ulusoy, 2008).

More complexities as their membership status in the European Union brought them to interact with the organization that also seeks to solve the problem. Greece became part of the EU in 1981. Cyprus joined the union in 2004 while Turkey remained a candidate for the EU while being scrutinized for the democracy, human rights, and freedom values. At some point, both Cyprus and Turkey were candidates for the EU, but while Cyprus' position changed to being a member with the terms that the Cyprus issue was not a necessary condition for membership, Turkey's candidacy has been questioned severely and challenged in its inconsistency on its democratization process as well as human rights and freedom (Christou, 2002).

As a result of the two memberships in the EU, the organizations have been argued to lean toward the demands of its members in dealing with the issue of Cyprus. Such absence of neutrality has been observed since Greece joined the EU. The evidence of this is that all the EU interaction with Turkey about its accession, the issue of Cyprus or the Mediterranean at large passes through the Greece and Cyprus membership who can either allow or disallow such interaction with Turkey. Although the Turkish government tries to separate issues in a manner that will make resolution easier in each areas of contention, especially with regard to the ascension to the EU. Nevertheless, being a part of the European Union is hinged on the resolving of the Cyprus problem (Eralp & Beriker, 2005).

This is a point where Turkey can be obliged to amend its stand in Cyprus in exchange for becoming an EU member. However, the discovery of hydrocarbon on the Mediterranean shores of Cyprus has made Turkey hold fast to its position in Cyprus with an attempt to benefit from the gas discovery.

*1.3.2.1. Political Interference and Energy: Impediments to Conflict Resolution*
Since South Cyprus claimed to be a Republic of Cyprus (RoC), it had the jurisdiction, also known as de facto recognition with its membership in the United Nations and European Union, necessary to extract the oil. At the same time, it is anticipated that the income made from the energy would be split between the Northern and Southern Cypriots, also known as Turkish and Greek Cypriots, respectively. This has been the stance of the international community during this whole process. In retaliation to the normative acceptance of the Greek Cypriot government as the exploiter, the Turkish Republic of Northern Cyprus (TRNC) administration has countered by concurrently exploring oil blocks to which they are entitled. The Turkish have also asserted their right to export goods. According to Gürel et al. (2013), the RoC must take a break from the further debate

overexploiting this liquefied natural gas, and Turkey cannot participate in the pipeline's building (Gürel et al., 2013).

On the contrary, Taliotis et al. (2014) make an effort to consider the energy sector's monetary implications in addition to the required time. Cyprus has been going through a financial crisis, and the discovery of this gas and oil is an opportunity to capitalize on. To begin, it will provide a substitute for importing such energy, referred to as an import replacement approach, which has the potential to improve industrialization procedures. Second, industrialization will free up space for an additional 200 billion $m^3$ of natural gas. The engagement with multinational firms like Total, Kogas, and Noratek was carried to the next level. The author agrees that political procedures determine how the product will be sold by exploiting the resource.

The outcome demonstrates that Cyprus is capable of raising cash for natural gas, which will result in a shift in how the island generates electricity. As soon as there is any kind of industrialization, there will be significant progress. Because of its substantial natural gas reserves, Cyprus has the potential to become a central nation in both the Mediterranean and the Middle East and North Africa (MENA) area. The Middle East and North African nations would turn to Cyprus as a source of information on how the income distribution from the exploitation of hydrocarbons would be divided. The Greek Cypriot authorities who were questioned demonstrated their openness and comprehension toward the advantages that may be shared by both sides. They are reflective of a perspective that seeks to share resources as well as the financial ramifications of doing so. In addition to this, they see hydrocarbon as a means to an end, a path toward resolving the dispute that has been going on for over 30 years (Taliotis et al., 2014).

An interesting element that is related to the reality that powerful politics may not be beneficial if used alone is that it disqualifies the idea of power politics, hard bargaining, and zero-sum game as "the only game in town" in terms of hydrocarbon. This is a fascinating component that pertains to the fact that high politics may not be a good means since it is employed alone. As an alternative to the war in Cyprus over lands and property, economic and financial mutual advantages are beginning to emerge as a potential solution. The hydrocarbon will result in a common aim for mutual benefit, despite political hard bargains, according to a Greek official at the United Nations. This is the prediction made by the official in the event that a political solution cannot be achieved. One of the most prominent tendencies in the viewpoint of the Greek Cypriots is that they strive to protect Turkish Cypriots from falling into the hands of Turkey while at the same time drawing them closer to themselves. This indicates that Greek Cypriots use language that limits the parties involved in the conversations to solely Greek Cypriots and Turkish Cypriots.

As a direct result of this, the Turkish Cypriots on their side have not yet acknowledged the RoC as being reserved exclusively for the Greek Cypriots. As a result, each and every agreement and decision that the Greek Cypriots made in their capacity as the only representation of RoC has been contested. This includes the Greek Cypriot government's compromise on the Exclusive Economic Zone (EEZ) with the governments of third-world nations over hydrocarbon licensing;

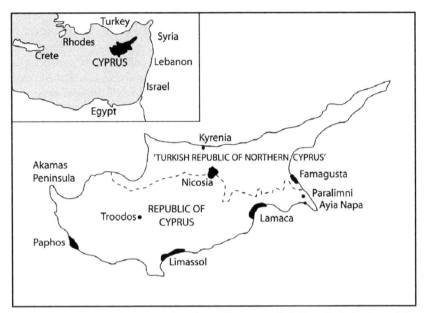

Fig. 1. *An Island Split in Two*: Southern Cyprus, officially called the Republic of Cyprus (Greek Cyprus), is a state and member of the United Nations and the European Union, producing natural gas off its coast. While Northern Cyprus, officially called the Turkish Republic of Northern Cyprus (TRNC), is an unrecognized region with about 40,000 Turkish troops. *Source*: Alipour et al. (2011).

this would merely imply that the Greek Cypriots are taking actions and signing a contract on an asset that does not exclusively belong to them. The Turkish Cypriots have the perception that they are entitled to certain privileges inside the RoC. If a political solution is not found, the Turkish Cypriots will not acknowledge the right of the Greek Cypriots to sign an agreement relating to the EEZ. If such a step were taken, the Turkish Cypriots would be left without a voice in the matter of the hydrocarbons. The author referred to the situation as a "done deal" while attempting to explain how the Turkish Cypriots felt.

As a direct consequence of this, they have maintained the position that the problem of offshore mineral resources must be put on hold until the political issues are settled. The Turkish Cypriots have expressed optimism that the hydrocarbon problem may be resolved via the implementation of a federal system.

These demonstrate that money is necessary, but there are other requirements in addition to sovereignty. Therefore, it has been suggested that Turkish Cypriots placed a higher priority on discussions of sovereignty than discussions of oil resources. This indicates that the problem of hydrocarbons may be readily handled after the problem of sovereignty has been resolved. According to Gürel et al. (2013), Turkish Cypriots will be able to exploit hydrocarbon resources regardless of whether or not they have sovereignty if they have a broader view of sovereignty, which includes marine rights.

*1.3.2.2. Reciprocated Exploration*
Historiographically speaking, the beginning of the 21st century represented the commencement of the negotiating process for Greek Cypriots operating on behalf of the RoC. This marked the beginning of a phase of collaborative growth in the hydrocarbon process with neighbors such as Egypt and Syria. It was made clear in a number of exchanges of communication that the TRNC does not recognize the legality of the EEZ delimitation agreements that Greek Cypriots signed with Lebanon. Mehmet Ali Talat said that such accords cannot be deemed genuine since the Turkish Republic of Northern Cyprus does not represent the whole island, and similarly, Greek Cypriots who rule the Republic of Cyprus cannot represent the entire island. The case of the offshore hydrocarbons and delimitation signatories is said to further aggravate the already tense relationship that exists in the area. This is another line of reasoning.

Despite this, the conflict with Cyprus continues to be one of the concerns contributing to the area's difficulty. The connection between Greek and Turkish Cypriots' governments continues to deteriorate due to the continued support that Greek Cypriots (as RoC) get from the international community. The recognition of South Cyprus as the recognition of their government in 2004 as RoC in the EU has further complicated the issue as it was brought to the attention of the EU. As a result of the position taken by the EU, most states are motivated to negotiate a delimitation deal with the GC/RoC. In 2010, Israel participated in this act when it announced the discovery of hydrocarbons in its territorial seas. For Israel, some writers have suggested that if the hydrocarbons of Cyprus and Israel are handled correctly, it might lead to a power re-arrangement in that area, bringing stability to Cyprus. This argument was made about the hydrocarbons of Cyprus and Israel (Taliotis et al., 2014).

A type of reciprocity may be said to have been shown by the TC/TRNC in reaction to the GC/RoC's activities. Since the Greek Cypriots had already begun signing deals with its neighbors, the Turkish Republic of Northern Cyprus (TRNC) also gradually began to form agreements with parties interested in the hydrocarbon and started exploring for it. This is the fundamental idea behind the concept of reciprocity. The suggestions put up by Turkish Cypriots were shot down by Greek Cypriots in the past since the Greek Cypriots have a stronger position because of the recognition they have received from the international world.

As a result, the TRNC, in order to further the interests of Turkish Cypriots, started exploring. They were giving a warning that in the event that the South and its allies took military action, the North would be prepared to respond with the support of Turkey to any assault of this kind. Both Turkish Cypriots and Turks living on the mainland have maintained that this should be the basis for the use of force while defending the idea of guarantorship. Due to the fact that this level of safety could be guaranteed, the TRNC started its research in the year 2012. Before beginning the exploration, a proposal about the hydrocarbon solution was presented to the United Nations. This was done in preparation for the exploration.

> The Turkish Cypriot proposal is for the Turkish Cypriot and Greek Cypriot sides to agree, without prejudice to their legal and

political positions on the Cyprus problem, on a place concerning the activities related to the hydrocarbon deposits off the coastlines of the island of Cyprus. (Gürel et al., 2013)

This proposal was found in Gürel et al.'s article.

In the end, the substance of the idea implies that the United Nations would take the lead in establishing a team that would bring about the approval of both parties on an international convention concerning hydrocarbon and how to come to an agreement on sharing the returns from it. The plan said that the pipeline route via Turkey had been viewed as the most beneficial path to the parties' interest in the hydrocarbon. These parties include both Cypriot populations, as well as Greece, Turkey, and the EU.

*1.3.2.3. An Evaluation on Turkey and the Pipeline Routes*
In this regard, it is essential to assess Turkey's pipeline routes in conjunction with those of the other parties to determine whether there are actual advantages for the parties involved. The Nabucco pipeline is the most strategic and lucrative option for most parties engaged in the hydrocarbon resource. According to Pericleous (2012), if the majority of the hydrocarbon resource is to go via the Nabucco pipeline, then it would be in everyone's best interest to participate in the building of the pipeline.

In addition to this, the nations concerned have had a significant dependence on gas supplies from Russia. Due to the fact that Russia has frequently exploited this reliance as a bargaining chip in a variety of problems, Europe is unable to take a stand on issues concerning Russia's inappropriate behavior in international society for the long term. One such instance occurred in 2014 and 2022 in Ukraine, when Russia became involved in the conflict there. The possibility of Russia being hit with sanctions by the EU is one example of what may have caused the Russian government to contemplate cutting off its gas supply to Europe. Members of the European Union who are impacted by this scenario include Greece and the Republic of Cyprus.

The Nabucco pipeline is a configuration of the gas pipeline that runs from the border of Turkey and Bulgaria all the way to Baumgarten in Austria. In addition to the fact that it is the most lucrative route, proponents of this particular route also point to the fact that it provides a greater level of safety and is easier to distribute across Europe. The Greek Cypriots do have an option in the form of the way that goes via Rhodes Island; however, this route does not provide goods to Europe in a timely or secure manner. When compared to the Transatlantic Anatolian Pipeline (TANAP), which goes on as the Nabucco pipeline, the waters in such regions are too deep to pass through. This indicates that it obtains supplies from TANAP and from Ceyhan, which, due to the shallowness of its waters, provides a safe maritime route; in the meanwhile, the gas will be moved from the Karpas peninsula in Cyprus.

Exporting the natural gas in liquid form is one of the options available from the Greek Cypriot side of the proposed Nabucco pipeline. In order to do this, liquid plants in both the host country and the destination state will need to be liquidated and then de-liquidated. The process of converting from one state to another requires a significant investment of both cash and time. Because of this procedure, there will not be an immediate supply of gas since it must first go through the steps. Because of the increased amount of capital required, the price of gas per unit would be much higher than usual. – convert gas to liquid; – transfer liquid; – convert liquid to gas. Another option is building the offshore hydrocarbon gas field and connecting it to Cyprus and, from there, to the island of Rhodes and Europe through the mainland of Greece.

Pipeline construction will include cutting through seabed features not geographically favorable for the pipeline to connect the gas source and Cyprus. The fact that such a portion will still need to go into the EEZ of Turkey presents an additional obstacle. Even though all of these other options have been ruled out as possibilities, the Nabucco line has not been operational since 2010. The project is no longer being pursued since there are insufficient gas supplies. According to Pericleous (2012), this demonstrates that Turkey is a critical link in the most profitable distribution of gas.

The Turkish viewpoint may be broken down into two categories. In the first place, it denounces any kind of unilateral arrangement and authority over the hydrocarbon that the Greek Cypriots (RoC) have constructed based on the problem of Cyprus. The seas and marine zones that are considered to be Turkish property and that overlap with the European Economic Zone have been asserted by Turkey. They have contended that the agreement should not be valid since it was signed by just one party unilaterally. If a political solution can be found first, then a problem with hydrocarbons of this kind will be handled immediately. In a figurative sense, the solution that involves hydrocarbons will just be a band-aid for the Cyprus crisis, and we will still need to engage in serious political discussions.

It should not come as a surprise that this has a connection to the viewpoint of Turkish Cypriots. The Cyprus issue is still substantial, and as a result, it continues to have an impact on the status of the island, despite the fact that Turkey and Greece have had a number of other territorial disputes. Additionally, one could argue that Turkey ought to use its levers in order to speed up the process of becoming a member of the EU; but, Turkey would rather deal with the Cyprus problem while continuing to work in collaboration with the EU. Turkey has a good chance of winning the talks, and the concession it offers might be essential in finding a settlement. According to Pericleous (2012), the issue that still needs to be answered is "whether the Erdoan government will stand by its public commitment and demonstrate that it has the political will to reach a solution right now."

*1.3.2.4. Potential Reactions to Random Explorations*
As long as there is no agreement on how to divide the island's hydrocarbon resources between the two sides, Cyprus's future is open to a number of different scenarios. On the island of Cyprus, there are about six different scenarios that might play out.

To begin, Pericleous (2012) has made the case that Turkey may resort to the use of force to block the exploration if it is carried out in a region to which it also lays claim. He says this is likely to occur if the exploration is carried out in an area to which Turkey has also laid claim. According to Pericleous (2012), Turkey has said that it has rights over blocks 4, 5, 6, and 7, and it has threatened to use its military might to impede any activity on those blocks where it has declared the rights of Turkish Cypriots alongside the rights of Greek Cypriots.

Due to the evidence that was discovered in Block 12, Turkey is authorized to put a stop to the activities of any vessels that are currently participating in the exploration. The Turkish navy navigated around the Homer exploratory in order to obtain access to the boats that were conducting the exploration and to avoid being asked to leave the region. The limitation is that the nations or corporations researching the resource are not only the Republic of China (RoC), but also those with which the RoC has bartered and negotiated, such as France, Italy, and the United States. These nations possess strong military capabilities that allow them to compete effectively with the navy of Turkey. Because they are all members of NATO, which is another component that makes things more complicated, it is probable that the second instance won't be doable (Olgun, 2019).

Thirdly, regarding the resumption of discussions between Greek and Turkish Cypriots, it is possible that the elections for the Republic of Cyprus in 2013 would bring the parties back to the table. A fresh round of negotiations was also anticipated to result after the election in the TRNC in 2015. According to Pericleous, the only way this scenario may play out is if the victorious candidates had the goal of reunifying Cyprus in mind. The events that took place after the election provide enough evidence that both President Aknc and President Anastasiades are keenly interested in cooperating with one another in order to bring the nation back together. The Netherlands, along with other locations, played host to many rounds of negotiations. Despite the fact that these discussions have stalled or been put on hold as of late, it is still possible to reach a consensus and realize the goal of Cyprus's unification. The scenario calls for genuine discussions, but the issue has persisted owing to Turkey's meddling in the TRNC and the Aegean water boundaries and EU sanctions against Turkey (Kumar, 2020). One thing to keep in mind is that it was just a phase of the hard deal on the division of land.

Fourthly, in contrast to the reciprocal action of "explore, and I will do the same," if the income gained from the hydrocarbon is handled jointly, it will safeguard the environment. In this conversation between the South and the North, the subject of the atmosphere has not come up. In addition, the RoC did not engage in any hydrocarbon-related discussions with Turkish Cypriots throughout the year 2012.

Fifthly, in light of the failure of the most recent memorandum, holding a referendum will only be feasible for a limited time. It wasn't simply the referendum that caused the prolonged period of tension and finger-pointing; the defeat itself was also a contributing factor. Even if the administrations of both countries were to switch, there is little chance that things would alter much due to the fact that the Republic of Cyprus would only vote for a party that would take a strong stance with regard to the Turkish Cypriots (Pericleous, 2012).

Because the internal choices that have been made in Cyprus need to be addressed, a sixth and last alternative is to bring Israel as another player into the mix.

This sixth facet tells that the only oil block that is the most lucrative is block 12, and that it will be impossible to fund anything that is smaller than this block. Nevertheless, Turkey surrounds block 12, which is supported by Turkish Cypriots. As a result, the RoC is required to wait longer for the discovery of another block, which may come in at a higher level than block 12. The Republic of Cyprus has the option of allowing Israel to utilize the oil facility if Israel is willing to do so; but, doing so would still present a problem to Turkish Cypriots and the British, who are both legally entitled to the island's assets. As a result, Israel's willingness to conduct a certain number of operations in Cyprus is going to be severely restricted (Kumar, 2020).

Changes in Turkey's internal politics and the dramatic unfolding of events in the Middle East will, in the future, make it abundantly evident to us whether or not Israel will choose to begin engaging with Turkey as an alternative to the RoC. As both nations fight to protect their mutual interests in the Syrian civil war and in maintaining regional stability, it is inevitable that ties between Israel and Turkey will strengthen. The notion that Israel sends its gas pipes via Turkey through the Trans-Anatolia pipeline and subsequently utilizes the Nabucco pipeline might be implemented if Israel chooses to do so. Pipelines may be transported across the European Economic Zone if Israel consults with the RoC.

### 1.3.3. Arab–Israeli Conflict

In addition to the perspective on hydrocarbon in the Mediterranean, the Arab–Israeli conflict which the Palestinian issue is a part of, also contributes to the struggle for gaining and controlling of resources in the region. Hence, beginning with the Palestinian–Israeli conflict, the point at which the problem started in regard to the hydrocarbon is Palestine and Israel, when the British Gas company discovered that there was gas in the Palestinian waters of Gaza. The Israeli government insisted that no construction of a gas marine field will take place across Gaza, except the British Gas is willing to pass through Israel and to make it the distributor of the gas. This proposal was rejected by the company considering the Palestinian people and their rights to their land and resources (Stocker, 2012).

The offshore oil across Gaza waters has therefore remained untapped and undeveloped as a result of such conditions that have been put forward by the Israeli government to become the key distributor of the gas that comes from the waters of Gaza. The problem persists in the separation of the Exclusive Economic Zone that is between Israel and Lebanon which is the annexation of Lebanese water of about 800 sq km (Khadduri, 2012).

Firstly, the discovery of gas in the Mediterranean attracted the Multinational Oil Corporations (MOC) to start looking toward the north-east of the Mediterranean for opportunities to drill and export oil along the coast in the region. In the last days of the 20th century, the British Gas received permission from the Palestinian Authority, of a 25-year opportunity to explore the Palestinian offshore for gas (Kostianoy & Carpenter, 2018).

A group of actors that includes the British Gas, Palestinian Investment Fund, Consolidated Contractors Company from Athens, and other small sub-actors formed a consortium which would undertake the drilling and exploring of the Gaza waters. The mission was to the construct the field and establish the pipelines that will be used for distribution from Gaza. This included the surveying of the offshore region of about 1,000 sq km and drilled wells that led to the establishment of the Gaza Marine Field.

This was approved by the Palestinian Authority in 2002 and expected that the exploration will begin four years after. This would replace the dependence of Gaza on the import of oil from Israel, by supplying Gaza directly from the marine field. This concession was set to begin in 2000 and end in the year 2025; however, it has remained unimplemented as the Israeli government disallowed such development in the region since it had requested that Israel should be the first partaker of the Gaza oil. Its suggestion was to ensure the oil bypasses Gaza by pumping to Israel while Israel continues to supply Gaza (Khadduri, 2012).

Considering the non-implementation of this first agreement, it has been argued that Israel's refusal has led to the undeveloped marine field. The development of this offshore oil would have contributed to the development of the Palestinian economy which would have led to its independence, at least for its own advantage. Scholars have argued that the Gaza offshore oil, which is part of the Mediterranean deposits, stands to give the opportunity to Palestine to become a strategic state that is needed by most countries around the world. The recognition of Palestine could have possibly been pushed forward by several actors (Chomsky & Papp, 2013).

Meanwhile, Israel's attempt to discover its own onshore petroleum started over five decades ago. It has struggled to find a field that can produce as much as can supply to other countries after meeting its own need. However, in the early years of the 21st century, it hit a field that provided sufficient for exportation. The energy discovery in Israel has added to its goods being exported, however it still imports about 80% of the energy it produces. This is because of the Israel's rejection of the Gaza exploration because of its adverse conditions (Ismail et al., 2013).

Much more to this is the Arab–Israeli conflict at large. Israel had experienced a high level of boycott from the Arab countries as a result of the Palestinian issue and other tensions that have grown in the region. With regard to gas exploration, international oil companies are refusing to work in Israel since their gas will be boycotted by many countries. Although drilling technologies have developed rapidly, it is also noteworthy that global oil companies work in other Arab countries, and therefore would not want to risk losing the opportunities to continue to explore in these countries because of the new and limited Israel's gas.

As a result, Israel has continued to make use of its local exploration companies with smaller facilities and experiences as well as focusing on the onshore drilling rather than offshore since it has disputed the case of Gaza offshore. Nevertheless, it has managed to explore 400 gas wells since it began to explore its gas. Despite all these, agreements among countries in the Mediterranean and the Middle East have granted the international oil companies the opportunity to shuffle between countries that have access to onshore or offshore gas. Because of the Camp David agreement which took place as a diplomatic relation between Egypt and Israel, the Arab countries have maintained sanctions (Antreasyan, 2013).

Another connected issue to the Arab–Israeli conflict regarding the hydrocarbon is the United States Noble Energy Mari-B fields. These fields are adjacent to the offshore deposit of the Palestinian waters. They were discovered almost at the same time that the Gaza offshore gas deposit was discovered and discussed. The Mari-B has been the most progressive field in this region having been discovered in 1998, while production started in 2004 and is expected to continue for the next 10 years. The early years of the new millennium were characterized by the importance of exploration for the region. The Palestinian Authority has claimed that the Mari-B zone within the region, the drilling exercise that has been taking place through horizontal drilling means that they have been accessing other offshore oil from whichever area they are undertaking drilling (Healy et al., 2012).

In 2009, another consortium under the leadership of Noble Energy with the inclusion of other local drilling companies from Israel discovered another oil field. This new field is located in Tamar at 90 km offshore from Haifa. The main part of this field is located on the southern offshore of Lebanon with a possible drilling exercise that started in 2013. This increased the supply of Israel's electricity through the Israeli Electric Corporation through gas.

Significance is that the consortium discovered the Leviathan field which has a significant level of reserves, however it is located in the direction of the Lebanese and Cypriot waters. These new regions discovered in the northern waters changed Israel's energy dependence as the gas will replace the soft coal that produces electricity as well as the natural gas that is imported from Egypt. Another advantage to Israel is that it provides it with the opportunity to export more gas that it would have previously not been able to explore considering the Gaza rejection. This will make Israel a new supplier of gas to the European states. Nevertheless, the Israeli government has suggested that it will produce and reserve sufficient gas for itself that will be sufficient to serve it for half a century (Fischhendler & Nathan, 2014).

Security discourse is introduced into the situation as there is a tendency that there will be attacks on the offshore drilling location. Israel's neighbors are to the south the Palestinians, and to the north Lebanon; therefore, any form of escalation of conflict will lead to the offshore field being a target. Also, if any of these countries extend their naval force operation toward the offshore field, this will affect the continuation of the oil exploration (Fischhendler, 2018).

Lebanon's political climate also adds to the region's hydrocarbon development. The country came late in its own exploration as it was only able to agree with the Norwegian government on the possibility of cooperation in providing logistics and experience with regard to the development of its oil and gas industry. Hence, Norwegian Petroleum Geo-Services began operations in 2007 with full authority to study the coast of Lebanon, Exclusive Economic Zone in the direction of Cyprus. The Lebanon and the Cyprus governments signed an agreement that stated the extent of the Exclusive Economic Zone. The non-implementation of this agreement is linked to the refusal of the parliaments to ratify the accord. Some have argued that Israel will push for their ownership of the Lebanese waters or that Turkey will push the country against its desire regarding hydrocarbon (Fattouh & El-Katiri, 2015).

The Lebanese and the Israeli governments decided to set the boundaries of the maritime offshore that they share and it was recognized by the United Nations as legal and binding. Nevertheless, Israeli empowered Noble Energy has continued the offshore exploration of oil and gas, and the tapping is reaching beyond the set Lebanon maritime boundary. Hence, Lebanon has continued to send legal warnings to Noble Energy informing it and warning it of the risk of tapping petroleum in the contested area or the areas that belong to Lebanon (Aoude, 2019).

***1.3.4. Lebanon and Israel: From a Long Conflict to an Agreement***

The conflict between Lebanon and Israel dates back to 1948 and the establishment of the State of Israel. Since then, Lebanon has not recognized Israel, and the struggle between them continues. The protracted conflict witnessed escalating events as the Palestinians used the Lebanese territory to launch attacks on Israel. Israel responded by launching attacks on the Palestinian forces in the Lebanese territory, occupying a large area of Lebanon. Amid these circumstances, the Lebanese resistance group and the Iranian proxy in Lebanon became active. Hezbollah, in the face of Israel, strengthened its position during the Lebanese Civil War and took control of southern Lebanon. Israel launched a war in 2006 against Lebanon in an attempt to uproot Hezbollah, which led to a further deterioration of the problem (Krhovska, 2014, p. 42).

The Security Council intervened and formally ended the hostilities following the Resolution No. 1701; a borderline called the Blue Line was established between the two countries. In reality, both countries rejected the line and did not recognize it. In other words, there has yet to be a final agreement on demarcating the borders between Israel and Lebanon. And since the maritime borders depend mainly on the land borders, the problems between the two countries have exacerbated, in light of the gas discoveries in the Eastern Mediterranean and the expansion of the disputed borders to include the maritime borders in addition to the land borders. In the wake of the beginnings of gas discoveries in the Eastern Mediterranean, Lebanon set geographical coordinates to delineate its exclusive economic zone.

Lebanon deposited those coordinates attached to maps with the Secretary-General of the United Nations in October 2010. In parallel, Israel also deposited the coordinates of its maritime borders with the United Nations, and it claimed that there is a section belonging to it within the exclusive economic zone drawn by Lebanon with an area of about 850 square kilometers, specifically Block No. 9 (Cohen & Boms, 2021).

It is also worth mentioning that Lebanon had signed an agreement with Cyprus to restrict the economic zone. The two-state agreement was concluded in 2007, and Cyprus ratified the agreement, while Lebanon did not.

On the other hand, Israel signed an exclusive economic zone agreement with Cyprus in October 2010, which was submitted to the United Nations. Lebanon strongly objected to that agreement, considering it illegal and violating Lebanese territorial waters. The matter even reached the point where the Lebanese Hezbollah directly threatened Israel to strike its ships and installations that are engaged in marine exploration activities if Israel encroaches on Lebanese waters) Krhovska, 2014, p. 42).

Lebanon has embarked on exploration operations in its exclusive economic zone, despite the ongoing conflict with its neighboring countries. The Israeli Minister of Defense commented in January 2018 that Lebanon had granted three foreign companies licenses to explore oil and gas as a "blatant challenge and provocative act." The Lebanese government responded with a series of strongly worded statements defending its rights, in addition to Hezbollah's announcement in the same month that it would confront any attack on Lebanese oil rights – a reference to Block No. 9 and confronting Israeli ambitions in Lebanon's resource, water and land (Cohen & Boms, 2021).

Finally, there is good news from the Middle East, and the world's media agencies have paid attention to it. Lebanon and Israel have reached an agreement on their water boundary and removed all obstacles to exploiting gas fields in the Eastern Mediterranean. After two years of US mediation efforts between Lebanon and Israel, the agreement was signed at the United Nations on October 11, 2022. Israeli Prime Minister Yair Labid said "We have reached a historic agreement. The agreement will strengthen Israel's security. We will have billions of dollars in economic growth because our northern border will be stabilized." The Lebanese presidency said in a statement that the final draft agreement was satisfactory and responded to Lebanon's wishes (CNBC, 2022).

The US envoy to the world energy Amos Hochstein prepared the final draft of the agreement, which Israel agreed to a month ago, and Lebanon has called for some changes. According to the agreement, the Karish gas field was a point of contention, which Israel believed was entirely within its waters and should not be negotiated. Lebanon claimed part of the field. However, Hezbollah has threatened to attack Israel if it invests in the field. According to the draft agreement, the field will be under Israeli control, while the Qana field will be given to Lebanon, although part of it is outside the border between Lebanon and Israel.

Chapter Two

# Oil and Natural Gas, Water Demarcation, and Electrification on the Mediterranean

## Abstract

The Eastern Mediterranean countries exhibit diversity in religion, culture, politics, and economy, amid rapid and dynamic regional developments shaped by global polarization and the international security landscape, rendering future prognostications challenging. This chapter delves into the realms of oil and natural gas production, the influx of multinational corporations, water boundaries, and renewable energy vis-à-vis fossil fuels in the Eastern Mediterranean, elucidating the realities of cooperation and competition within the region. Analysis of cooperation and competition dynamics is imperative for comprehending the tensions among states. Enhanced cooperation between states may lead to mutual benefits, such as increased oil and gas prices favoring their partnership, while any escalation in competition can swiftly be perceived as a threat, exacerbating tensions. The desirability of such cooperation or competition in the international political economy remains subject to ongoing debate.

*Keywords*: Oil; natural gas; multinational corporations; renewable energy; regional cooperation

## 2.1. International Political Economy of Oil and Gas

The examination of the political economy of the Mediterranean basin requires three major issues that are linked to the economic advantage of the Mediterranean. Oil will examine the interests of the major international oil companies, the oil pipeline project in the Mediterranean, and the number of countries that are intended to benefit from the terms of trade in the region. British Petroleum/Beyond Petroleum, Eni, an Italian multinational oil and gas company; Exxon

Mobil, an American multinational oil corporation; and Total, a French multinational integrated oil and gas company, are present in the areas to survey and examine the Mediterranean Sea for the feasibility of the profitability of the oil and natural gas.

The challenge they face is being locked into political conflicts between two nations. The section on oil and gas intends to argue that they are not external actors but rather part of the political disputes through the consent to survey the region given by the affiliated nations. For instance, during its activities in the region, Eni has been kneaded into the Israeli–Lebanon conflict as well as the Republic of Cyprus and Turkey. With the intention that every country's pursuit is to maximize their access to resources to meet their own needs, companies have been wrapped in political challenges and complexity (Özgür, 2017).

Oil has been regarded as the moving force of industrialized countries and has become the most significant energy source since the mid-20th century. All the resources generated from it have been used to create and power a modern society because it serves as a form of energy to heat homes, used in home products such as Vaseline, detergents, plastics, colors and paints, power vehicles, and vessels, fly planes, used to move goods from one point to another as well as in other fields such as medicine. The UKOG argued that oil caters to about 90% of the transport industry worldwide (UKOG, 2021). Furthermore, it has been statistically argued that over 1.6 trillion jobs have been created within a decade by the oil and gas industry and has helped families to make billions of profits. Due to the enormous use of oil and gas, there has been an increase in the development of infrastructure and research within the nation. The sufficient supply also results in costs worldwide (Yergin, 2020).

All these roles played by oil and gas within the national economy justify that they are majorly traded commodities in international trade. The economies of scale have allowed the transportation of these products to be easy and cheaper, making it flow through all the country's pipelines. Although the oil trade is at the global level and gas is regional, both commodities are sought after by all countries as they contribute to the balance of payment improvement in their current accounts.

## 2.2. Geopolitics of Oil

Geopolitics and oil are connected and are difficult to disentangle. The types of oil barrels in the region's market create a problem of oil price volatility because of the pattern which they use in determining price. For example, the wet barrel which is the physical purchase of crude oil always considered the paper barrel which is where the promises of the purchase of crude oil for the future have been made by states to predict the price of the oil; while the paper barrel considers the physical wet barrel market to examine the surplus and the shortage to predict the price of oil which determines where to invest (Stevens, 2004).

Hence, while the wet market is a function of economics, the paper market is a function of psychological perception to invest. Therefore, there is a problem of volatility. The volatility problem is a result of the lack of knowledge about the functioning of the oil industry. The oil-producing countries using the paper barrel market misread the economics of the wet barrel market, therefore, presuming that there is a possible shortage in the future in a situation that shows a surplus. In addition to the lack of knowledge about the market, sudden change in perception is another source of price volatility and the prices can also change alongside (Bacchetta & Van Wincoop, 2004).

Within the context of geopolitics, historical price records will be examined in light of the two causes of volatilities. The shortage of oil supply comes because of geopolitical occurrences which include conflicts, war, rumors of war, etc., and this affects the physical supply of oil in the region. It also affects the expectation within the promises of the supply of oil in the future. Other factors include government security policies. The security and assurance of the supply of oil propel the government energy policies and this affects their usage of the resource (Stevens, 2016). Furthermore, concerns about the security of supply propel the importing policies of the energy-importing states which also affects their consumption. The producers are also affected by the demand which affects the depletion policies of the producing states focusing on the rise or fall of the national resources. Hence, the struggle among states to gain access to the supply of oil to avoid any form of shortage on their sides, for the local use of exportation (Escribano, 2017).

### 2.2.1. The Implication of Uncertainty on Oil Geopolitics

The indicators on the future of the energy market show the development of new policies from different countries in the context of very uncertain energy prices. States are beginning to create geopolitical policies that include or exclude the other members of the region (Högselius, 2018). Hence, the perspective about the future consumption of oil that shapes the behavior of the state must be considered. The extent to which oil will be relevant begins with the strong consensus on the level of traveling in the future. The increase in travel will grow the demand for oil in non-oil producing countries, and oil nations with access to oil and gas will take advantage of this high demand to make an economic profit. The argument is that oil energy will continue to dominate the energy market supply. The reason for this assumption is that economic models of quantitative and qualitative research have shown the drivers of demand.

The COVID-19 period has shown how much citizens desire to move from one nation to other by every means of transport to carry out their businesses. The demand to stay indoors during the lockdown still shows a significant level of travel for business was not stopped. As a matter of fact, cargo flights were regularly on the move using oil and gas despite the drop in demand during this period. In the nearby future, the opening of borders will result in high transportation since people have been locked down for a long while. The countries that are new to the supply of oil and gas are looking forward to this growth in demand as an assurance of market for their supply (Correlje & Van der Linde, 2006).

The countries located in the eastern Mediterranean differ in terms of religion, culture, politics, and economy. Moreover, regional developments are rapid and dramatic because they are influenced by global polarization and the international security system, making it difficult to forecast what will happen tomorrow. An unexpected event may occur, causing the region's strategic plans to be canceled. For example, the three oil shocks that happened in 1973, the 1979 oil shock, and the 1986 oil crisis are results of the Mile Island issue to the Chernobyl, the nuclear-weapon use in Fukuyama, and the Macondo oil spillage. Technological changes also affect the supply and demand of oil and gas, while nevertheless the challenge of politically vested interest affects these factors (Friedman, 2011). The IEA, for instance, was established to convince the oil-importing countries to decrease their dependence on imported oil. Foreseeing the shortages in the future might be seen as an effective measure to caution states in the pursuit of oil and gas development to reduce competition and tensions.

Furthermore, Stevens (2016) proposes that forecasting the shortages of oil and gas will help the consumer government find an alternative source of energy. On the other side, oil-producing nations and oil companies are encouraging share-holders to make more investments by proving that there is increasing demand for more profitability. These show that both consumers and producers can create false expectations if they continue to run the business as usual.

First, it is necessary to progress by stating that states are still the main actors in the political economy, since all other actors perform their functions based on the state where its headquarters is located. Also, the state protects other actors that are registered in its territory and operate as global multinational corporations. Second, the power however is not limited to the state, as other actors such as the MNCs can shape the direction of the global political economy in a way that either weakens or strengthens the position of the state. Hence, the state tries to use MNCs to gain an advantage in the international economic system while threatening or sanctioning any MNC that intends to weaken its power or position (Biamouridis & Tsafos, 2015).

The political economy of oil and gas assures the state of their energy security, that they do lack regular access to the flow of oil which might affect the internal and external functioning of the states if those resources are not easily and abundantly accessible. To achieve this involves both cooperation and competition among the state, thereby creating friends and enemies in the oil and gas discourse (Schneider et al., 2014). Competition and cooperation exist concurrently in the political economy of oil irrespective of the antagonistic character that they exhibit. Political economic cooperation among states rests on the argument that believing in the capability to forecast and plan the future and mitigate the opportunity for other actors to become separate from the discourse.

Hence, they become automatically connected to the discourse without being sidelined. The political-economic competition focuses on the capability of a state to sideline another state in the context of having access to oil and gas. As a result, the political economy of the oil and gas market is continuously propelled by the tension between cooperation and competition. The implication of these will be examined after which empirical evidence will be presented on the conduct of states along with the MNCs (Moon & Lado, 2000).

The security assurance granted to the state by having access to oil and gas is regarded as energy security (Ruhl, 2010, p. 63). Based on the state-centric monopoly of the use of power, this access can be maintained using force. For instance, the Cater doctrine during the Cold War ensures that oil and gas are regularly supplied and the use of force is suggested as the means to sustain supply, especially from the Middle East. This has been carried out by the Carter Administration through military deployment and proxy wars to exploration sites on the sea where there are strategic resources (Le Billon, 2004).

Other examples of how a state has pushed for its energy security include the combination of principles that direct the conduct of states. These include competition, environment, and supply of resources, availability, accessibility, acceptance, and affordability (Umbach, 2016, pp. 96–97). This combination can be three or more to create an energy security model.

### 2.2.2. Cooperation and Competition in Oil-Producing Countries

The pattern in which states make these choices is subject to the means of achieving their energy security instead of the sustainability of the energy supply (Baumann, 2008). Irrespective of the variations among models, the common objective is to mitigate all forms of disruption in the flow of oil and gas toward the state. The supply must be convenient, uninterrupted, and unthreatened by any factor. For instance, the increase in oil prices does not stop the flow of oil, but the high prices can make the flow difficult, which will change the position of the state in influencing the political economy of oil and gas (Reed & others, 2016).

As a result, cooperation and competition discourse are necessary to understand the tension that occurs among states. If a particular state increases cooperation with another state, the increase in oil price by any of the two favors their partnership. However, a competing state quickly identifies this increase as a threat and tension rises. Whether this cooperation or competition is desirable in the international political economy remains a matter of debate (Fletcher, 2016).

In the case of OPEC's function as a mechanism for cooperation between its members and non-OPEC members, in 2014 this cooperation increased and arguably the previous position was, therefore, competition between the two groups. The cooperation ended with the hopes that oil prices can increase to the advantage of oil-producing countries. Impliedly, the prior struggle between OPEC members and non-OPEC oil-producing countries was non-cooperative, hence a competition. While that competition serves as an advantage to the non-producing countries, the cooperation serves as an advantage to the oil-producing countries. This is because OPEC has stated that its goal was to eliminate all other producers from the oil market and maintain increased production irrespective of the fall in prices (BBC, 2014).

OPEC's goal since its inception is to compete in the market as an organization against any non-OPEC suppliers' members. The change in strategy did not happen suddenly, but because of interaction with the non-OPEC oil producers. It has been argued that this cooperation is a defeat, as it changes the objective of OPEC to eliminate other producers; however, the understanding that competition and cooperation are not permanent provides consolation to such an argument (Street, 2016). The fluctuation in cooperation and competition is also recognized which could show a high level of competition as against cooperation or vice-versa.

*2.2.2.1. Cooperation and Competition of the Oil Companies*
Another aspect of cooperation and competition can be found in the environmental issue. Rather than focusing on states or oil-producing countries, the popular campaigns and oil and gas multinational corporations are also involved in competition and cooperation in the exploration of oil and gas. The environmentalists have campaigned for the collective divestment of all resources on the use of fossil fuels (Fossil Free, 2015). The campaigns have a financial impact on the oil operation of the MNCs. There have been several correspondences between the environmentalists and oil-producing companies like Exxon Mobil which have changed how they function. Exxon Mobil has been reprehensive in its response to these campaigns against its fossil fuel operation by the environmentalists because of the withdrawal of funding by significant investors. As a result, Exxon Mobil had no choice but to become cooperative with the environmentalists to negotiate their demands and move toward more environmentally friendly exploration. The campaigns also affect OPEC, and it has responded to cooperate to strengthen its position as an oil producer to minimize opposition from the environmentalist campaigns.

The cooperation shows that countries, companies, and international organizations are all involved in the cooperation and competition in the oil and gas discourse and therefore are part of the energy political economic game. Within the Mediterranean discourse, these elements; countries, companies, and international forums, are also present as well as different forms of cooperation and competition among them (Escribano, 2017).

## 2.3. The Political Economy of Hydrocarbon in the Eastern Mediterranean

Before the encounter with Eni, Exxon Mobil was ready to drill a natural gas well in the eastern Mediterranean Sea, off the coast of Cyprus; however, Turkey's Ministry of Energy and Natural Resources released a statement warning oil companies to consider drilling in that area to consider the political state of things and act following that. This statement refers to a caution not to drill since a political dispute is ongoing on the access in the region. Although it reflects a diplomatic tone, the message is obvious (Kontos, 2018).

The increase in gas discoveries off the coasts of Egypt, Israel, and Cyprus, led by international energy companies including Houston's Noble Energy, Royal Dutch Shell, and Exxon, are inflaming tensions in an already volatile region now facing the huge influx of resources that emanates from the region of Mediterranean. After Israel declared the need for an oil partner on the Mediterranean, Noble announced its Aphrodite field off the coast of Cyprus, holding 4.5 trillion cubic feet of gas. Three years later, Eni announced the Zhor field off the coast of Egypt, with an estimated 21.5 trillion cubic feet of gas. Right now, all eyes are on Exxon's exploratory wells off Cyprus, the results of which are expected to be publicized (Perrin, 2017).

The Texas oil giant has already floated the idea of building an LNG export facility in Cyprus, should the wells prove as prolific as hoped. Israel, Egypt, and Cyprus announced earlier that they had formed a joint group to develop the infrastructure necessary to move gas out of the Eastern Mediterranean, a region lacking in the LNG terminals and pipelines necessary to move gas to markets in Europe and Asia (Caswell et al., 2016).

How has Exxon Mobil, which went ahead with its plans, has so far avoided trouble, and what is the possibility of an attack breaking out in the Eastern Mediterranean over the drilling of oil that has been approved by one country but disapproved by another? The answer to this question can be straightforward, but the impact will be a lasting one on countries and companies. The Mediterranean Sea does not hold a part of the sole sovereignty of a state except for its shore areas. Hence, an attack on it might not mean an attack on the sovereignty of a state; however, the attack on the vessel of a country highlights a high level of aggression toward it. The attack on the company's operation or presence in the region is higher aggression toward a state and will lead to escalation (Tastan & Kutschka, 2019).

Although the aggression will be directed at the oil company, it may lead to war between the country that owns the company and the aggressor. To make this happen, a justifiable power match-up is required. Turkey is unlikely to interfere with American businesses for fear of inciting the US military. However, it may disrupt the operations of Total, a French oil company that has partnered with Eni on a contract to drill in Cypriot waters claimed by Turkey (Gürel & Cornu, 2013).

In addition, the geopolitical uncertainty and the possibility of military action could make obtaining the financing required to develop the offshore gas fields difficult. Financial institutions are unwilling to invest in the region after observing the level of tension which might make them lose their capital. Banks have drawn banks from pushing loans into the exploration of the Mediterranean region (Masuda, 2007).

Despite low natural gas prices during the discoveries of the reserves in the region in 2011, and uncertainty surrounding large offshore projects, the vast amounts of gas in the Eastern Mediterranean have transformed the region into one of the world's most active exploration areas. Nonetheless, oil and financial companies are skeptical about the issue. The company's action has been slowed as a result of repeated obstruction. Companies must notify their affiliated countries that grant drilling permission of their decision to postpone drilling operations due to political conflict. Nonetheless, the companies will not cancel the drills' capital expenditures (Legrenzi & Momani, 2011).

Before the spread of Coronavirus over the world, the Italian and French companies, Exploration by Eni and Total were scheduled to begin at the start of the year 2021 in the Block 6 section of the Mediterranean water; while ExxonMobil was scheduled to begin exploration in September 2021 in the Block 10. However, all these explorations have been postponed due to the COVID-19 pandemic that led to the downturn of the global economy. More specifically, the drop in oil prices, the rivalry between oil-producing countries such as Saudi Arabia and

Russia, and the failure of the OPEC and non-OPEC countries to collectively address oil production have led to the rescheduling of the exploration.

The drop in oil prices does not favor oil-producing states since the global economy relies mostly on oil production. The economic downturn and tension among oil-related economies would affect the newly discovered countries and their planning to explore their oil deposits in the Mediterranean since they see the already-producing countries as potential partners and clients (Arslan, 2020; Daily Sabah, 2020). The challenge is that, with the world's new direction toward renewable energy, how relevant will oil and its price be to these countries? The argument is that the issue of environmental matters in the Mediterranean might begin to accommodate greener environmental activities or changes in the global political economy's dynamics of oil. Therefore, depending on oil and gas might be a challenge. Whether this will change the direction of the pursuit of oil and gas remains questionable.

## 2.4. Water Resources Among Mediterranean Countries

The waters of the Mediterranean are characterized by features that show similarities and differences across the Mediterranean countries in the north and south. It is argued that water resources are unevenly distributed across time and space in the Mediterranean. For example, 90% of the water generated on the sea each year moves toward the north, while only 10% moves toward the south. This already creates an opportunity for a comparative advantage, triggering a political move. The coastal areas attract tourists from landlocked countries; however, there are variations in the level of civilization, urbanization, and industrialization in the coastal region of the Mediterranean countries. The region's challenge is the increase in the natural population growth and concentration in the coastal areas and the establishment of large cities on the Southern and Eastern Mediterranean coastline. Hazards such as prolonged drought or flooding create socio-economic constraints within the region, which have political implications (Burak & Margat, 2016).

Collectively among Mediterranean countries, there is the problem of imbalance between the population influx and decrease in the availability of freshwater resources. The water demands as well as water imports, non-conventional water production which includes desalinization has tripled in the same pattern with the population increase. Water needs in the Mediterranean are determined according to the requirements of the activities and the supply of water conditions which are mainly taken over by renewable natural water and resources that are gotten from the precipitation, fossil water extraction of both conventional and non-conventional. The regional evidence shows that there are increasing future demands for these water resources which are only accessible to the countries that have rights to sufficient areas of the Mediterranean seas. There has been a struggle on the seas as evidence shows that there is an increase in water exploitation. This signals the tension and competition among the countries in the Mediterranean. Hence, the discussion on the demarcation of the water, how political strategy is being used to argue for the rights to the Mediterranean is necessary (La Jeunesse et al., 2016).

## 2.4.1. Demarcation of Water: Another Wetland in the Mediterranean Region

The waters of the Mediterranean can be divided into two shores: the northern and the southern. The countries on the northern shore include Spain, Italy, Greece, Slovenia, Croatia, Bosnia-Herzegovina, Montenegro, Albania, and Turkey, while the southern shore countries are Syria, Lebanon, Israel, Palestinian Territories, Egypt, Libya, Tunisia, Algeria, and Morocco with Cyprus and Malta in the middle Mediterranean (Burak & Margat, 2016).

To consider the demarcation in light of all the countries is a broad spectrum however; focusing on the Northern Mediterranean countries and more specifically the Eastern Mediterranean which will include Greece, Turkey, Cyprus, Syria, Libya, and Egypt. Furthermore, to focus and streamline the demarcation to the tension in the region; Greece, Turkey, and Cyprus have been the most ardent adversaries on the demarcation of waters (De Guttry, 1984).

The demarcation of water is another issue that provides political advantages for countries and vessels that companies gain access to the assets in the waters as well as aid traveling. This conflict of the area of states jurisdiction on the seas is as old as the state themselves. The law of the sea seems not to have resolved this conflict leading to confrontations and interjecting of vessels by the state who claim their territorial waters sovereignty have been violated. The section into the power of the United Nations Convention on the Law of the Seas (UNCLOS) in 1994 has arranged the meaning of oceanic boundaries and opened the opportunities for states to guarantee the advantage of abusing assets far away from their territory regions. The "crawling purview" of the oceans has helped resolve old debates, yet in addition, revived others and made new ones. This section on water demarcation will examine the claims of states on the seas and occurrences of interjections concerning the law of the sea and the political games in the Mediterranean. This will involve thorny legal questions that would involve the interpretation of legal documents (Chevalier & Officer, 2004).

The territorial waters, continental shelves, and Exclusive Economic Zones of countries according to the International Law are blurry areas to define which results in tension among states that attempt to control the rich resources that are within their waters. It has been argued that this is what shapes the conflict in the Mediterranean between Turkey and Greece. The major tension in the Mediterranean of this sort is between Greece, Turkey, and Cyprus. To begin with historical landmarks, there has been an apprehensive attitude and contention between the two countries for 50 years over the Aegean Sea. While Greece continues to present agenda on the maritime delimitation agreement for the continental shelf with an EEZ around the Aegean Sea, Turkey has continued to involve a list of issues that seem unresolvable. For instance, the sovereignty of Turkey over some islands, demilitarization of other islands including Cyprus, the delimitation of the seas around Greece, and the question of the width of Greece's national airspace (Stocker, 2012).

Delimitation is the process by which there is a division of the maritime areas given that two states are competing over the ownership according to international law.

It might, for both parties, restrict the perceived sovereign rights. All these matters have been brought forward to the International Court of Justice, the Security Council, and other organizations such as the Council of Europe (Grigoriadis & Belke, 2020).

Under Article 121 of the Law of the Sea Convention, there is a difference between islands that belong to all maritime zones, and the rocks which are part of territorial seas or contiguous zone depending on the state in question. It is generally accepted that customary law provides for this distinction. Also, these performances are binding upon all parties, whether they are members of the Law of the Sea Convention or not. This is because customary international law practices have been argued to exist before the treaties and conventions (Kaye, 2017).

The challenges are not only what the island has inside of them but the impact on the maritime delimitation. Both countries agree that the islands do generate maritime zones, but they vary on how the eventual delimitation borderline would be drawn. The established rule with regards to the territorial sea delimitation which is the Article 15 LOSC and customary practices is regarded as the median line and in exceptional cases, there could be an adjustment. Both countries accept the fact that these islands and maritime delimitation are special circumstances and that it is getting tenser when it involves the delimitation of continental shelf and EEZ because there is no practical rule from LOSC articles that address this sui generis (Stocker, 2012).

Concerning the territorial seas of the Greek waters which is the width of the territorial waters, according to Article 3 of the LOSC and the customary practices of the state, all coastal states may have territorial waters that extend to 12 nautical miles away from the baselines. Customarily, the state is responsible for declaring the extent of its territorial seas unilaterally which is also provided in the LOSC. While Greece has not been one of the supporters of the United Nations Convention on the Law of the Sea at the beginning, it has become one of the countries that consistently reserved its rights to go beyond the current territorial sea's width of 6 nautical miles (Kalkan, 2020).

On the other hand, Ankara has continually disagreed with any kind of extension of Greece's territorial seas in the Aegean Sea. During the negotiation of the UNCLOS III, Ankara suggested an additional draft that proposes that the states' borders are enclosed and semi-closed seas which should be used to determine the width of the territorial seas by collective agreement. This position is restated by arguing that Turkey does object to the development of all forms of customary rule that are in line with Article 3 of the LOSC. Therefore, the extension of the Greek territorial sea is an abuse of rights, since it does not allow Turkey being one of the countries to the Aegean Sea, having the right to access the high seas through its territorial waters for economic and research purposes (Korkut, 2017).

As the struggle between the two countries continued, the intervention of the Council of Europe through the Council of Ministers became necessary. The body negated the objections of Turkey and established a decree of the Council of Ministers based on the Territorial Sea Act 2674 which maintained those Turkish territorial seas around the Black Sea and on the Mediterranean remain

12 nautical miles with the perspective of the principle of equity. Nevertheless, Turkey has continued to invoke different principles such as "casus belli," a justification for war, and acts to reflect this in its conduct. Although resorting to war has become unpopular among the states, provocations are ongoing from both sides on all territorial seas (Nathanson & Levy, 2012).

Deliberations on the territorial sea in the Greek Aegean Sea will continue to surface as one of the areas in negotiations directly or indirectly. For instance, the delimitation agreement between Italy and Egypt brought about the discussion of the 12nm of the Greek territorial waters while the Greek Foreign Minister was honoring the diplomatic event. The minister argues that they have to be in uniformity in the application of the territorial waters in the Greek zones and its border with Turkey will not be an exception (Grigoriadis & Belke, 2020).

After the Greek and Egyptian foreign ministers signed an agreement with regard to the Mediterranean maritime border, the Greek parliament ratified it. The success of this agreement is traced to the clause within the agreement that Greek islands possess continental shelves as well as exclusive economic zones unlike the argument of Turkey that Greece only has national waters. The two countries agreed to begin this form of partial demarcation which will become a whole piece to achieving full demarcation in further negotiations. Such negotiations have not taken place between Greece and Turkey, since the continental shelves and exclusive economic zones have not been agreed upon. Turkey is not a member of the United Nations Convention on the Law of the Sea; hence maritime demarcation with Greece is not possible (Marghelis, 2021).

Turkey on its side has entered into a defense and cooperation agreement with the Libyan Tripoli-based government regarding the exploration of the Mediterranean. The current situation in Libya does not give an assurance to this memorandum of understanding, since there are two governments in Libya with elections approaching which might affect the clauses in the memorandum. Whosoever wins the Libya election and leads in the determination of the future of the country will determine if the defense and cooperation with Turkey will remain (El Tawil, 2020).

Beyond the territorial sovereignty of states, the water demarcation issue has extended to other areas of the interaction between the states. These include concerns about the sovereignty of land and the natural features; the 10 nm airspace being used to demilitarize the group of islands in the Aegean which are related to the land sovereign as well as the sea and air of the two countries. Each of these countries has engaged in the revisionist analysis of different international agreements and treaties as a political means to push forward arguments according to the principles that support their dominance. It shows the loose commitments and interpretation of an international agreement about sovereignty since the development of the international system in the post-World War II period. Historically, the delimitation acrimony between Greece and Turkey started in the 1970s and has spilled over to the Aegean issue which is traceable to the last decade of the last century. Its development into expanding a grey aspect regarding sovereignty has put the countries' international borders at the risk of conflict (Institut Montaigne, 2020).

## 2.5. The Electrification of the Mediterranean Region

The electrification of the Mediterranean will be focused on renewable energy alongside oil and gas. The dimension of the energy sector will affect the direction of the political relations between countries and the economic advantage between multinational companies. The two dimensions of energy will be the use of clean energy generated through solar power or the continuous production in the oil and gas industry. The question is whether oil and gas are sustainable as the world is turning toward a green environment and clean energy. The invention of electric cars and solar energy may redirect the electrification of the Mediterranean toward using these alternative sources of energy.

However, the current state is still pursuing the use of oil and gas for electrification. Nevertheless, the general perspective is that the electrification of the Mediterranean is still an area of low politics as compared to the sharing of resources in the region. This area is rarely discussed in the issue of the Mediterranean. This section will focus on how such neglected areas which have been regarded as "low political issues" can affect the direction of the states in that region (Zachariadis & Hadjinicolaou, 2014).

Sustainable electrification of the Mediterranean involves the need for cooperation of the major local players about the hydrocarbon reserves and the possibility of electricity generation companies of each country in the region to build capacity for synergizing hydrocarbon and solar energy. Furthermore, the technological demands as well as the commercialization for profitability and the financial implication of such collaboration in the region signal areas of possible cooperation beyond the competition in the region. Consequently, energy projects, workshops, training exhibitions, and conferences will bring the countries together to improve cooperation. These areas are therefore significant; since they do not bring about the confrontations and tensions that are observable in the aspect of the drilling of oil and gas, territorial waters, and exclusive economic zones, as well as lands and properties. These are being regarded as "low politics can therefore become the bedrock on which real political issues can be solved" (Poullikkas et al., 2013).

By showing that the contestation on the Mediterranean for oil, natural gas, territorial waters, and the use of water to generate electricity provokes moves, actions, and reactions from several states to reposition themselves so as to win in the region: The Turkish government's move of sending a seismic research vessel escorted by a military fleet to examine the areas of the Mediterranean Sea claimed by Greece is one of the actions that have heightened the tension in the region in the last years. The result was a reactionary move from Greece and the European powers by responding to cause a military escalation. The military escalation transformed into de-escalation and the willingness to engage in exploratory talks among parties. These have examined each issue; oil and gas, water demarcation and electrification, and the actions of states in the context, the exploration of oil and natural gas, disputed territorial sovereignty, and the use of the seas.

Chapter Three

# The Regional Chessboard in the Eastern Mediterranean: A Call for Superpower

## Abstract

Since 2010, the eastern Mediterranean has witnessed a transformative narrative with the discovery of natural gas reserves off the coasts of Cyprus and Israel. This pivotal development has drawn attention to the region, where Egypt, Israel, Cyprus, Turkey, and Greece share maritime borders. The emergence of natural gas has reshaped geopolitical dynamics, and Western countries assume to reduce their reliance on Russia for energy supplies. This chapter explores the magnitude of natural gas discoveries and production in Cyprus and Israel, examining the interconnection of their fields and the ambitious endeavor of laying a 1,900-km underwater pipeline to the Greek island of Crete. Additionally, it highlights the pivotal roles played by key regional actors such as Israel, Turkey, and Egypt in shaping security and energy negotiations. However, Turkey has a significant position in the eastern Mediterranean and the Middle East, but tensions have arisen as neighboring countries seek to limit Turkey's involvement in regional energy discussions, viewing its policies as a potential threat, thereby exacerbating Turkey's regional interventions, particularly in Cyprus. Each of these countries in the Middle East is struggling to get more of the cake. Above all, Israel has been a gas importer throughout its history and now dreams of becoming a natural gas exporter to Europe.

*Keywords*: Gas exports; trilateral partnerships; Cyprus; Egypt; Israel

---

Deciphering the Eastern Mediterranean's Hydrocarbon Dynamics:
Unravelling Regional Shifts, 41–62
Copyright © 2024 by Bahrooz Jaafar Jabbar
Published under exclusive licence by Emerald Publishing Limited
doi:10.1108/978-1-83608-142-520241004

## 3.1. Israel's Mediterranean Pipedream: From Importing to Exporting Gas

Geo-strategy is a key determinant of economic priorities in the Eastern Mediterranean region. Countries inhabiting this region enjoy unique status regarding the presence of hydrocarbons, while the ability for these countries to maintain their individual positions yet not undermining regional co-operation still remains topical (Ratner, 2016). The developing regional order in the Eastern Mediterranean vis-à-vis the huge presence of hydrocarbons is an accurate representation of a symbiotic relationship between the different stakeholders in the region and their quest to maximize to the fullest, their energy capacities as major energy producers and consumers as well as positioning themselves at the top of the economic and political ladder of the region. In contrast, a shift from oil to gas is a vital part of this emerging order.

A reassessment of the cooperation between states within and without this region has become vital for consideration (Shaltami, 2020). Ascertaining the impacts of the political economy of hydrocarbons in the Eastern Mediterranean is the vein of this book; for that, uncovering the dynamics used by different stakeholders in obtaining and maintaining their fair share of the energy in the region as well as their geopolitical positioning will be examined:

When Israel became recognized as a state in 1948, its rating on the global political and economic scale was pinned to one word, "liability." Accordingly, in the most succinct expression, the new state was considered as weak and potentially vulnerable (Mearsheimer & Walt, 2006). Israel was in every way in a lack of energy resources and it hugely relied on foreign markets for importing energy produce such as coal, gas, and oil. That notwithstanding, time has altered to the different narrative as Israel is now perceived not only as valuable but as a strategic player in the global sphere of hydrocarbons. A significant advancement of Israel's energy affluence is characterized by its transition from an energy-importing country to a self-sufficient energy producer, consumer, and prospective exporter. This unprecedented leap in Israel's energy priority could be best described as "Israel's gas revolution."

It is common knowledge that Israel's current political and economic importance is tied to the presence of an enormous quantity of offshore gas in Israel. A handful of significant discoveries of natural gas fields have been made in Israel; such as the Tamar, Leviathan, Tanin, and Karish gas fields. Among these gas discoveries, one of the most significant is the Leviathan gas field discovered in 2010. With the Leviathan's discovery along with other gas fields, Israel has been flagged as a prospective and a potential gas exporter in the Eastern Mediterranean (Akyener, 2016). In December 2010, the Leviathan gas field was discovered offshore Israel which is presumably one of the largest offshore gas fields in the world.

While the US Geological Survey (USCG) estimated in 2010 that the Levant Basin contained a mean probable of 3.5 trillion cubic meters (tcm) of natural gas and of 1.7 billion barrels of recoverable oil (Tsakiris et al., 2018), the significance of this great discovery to Israel is multifaceted. Firstly, it removes Israel from the list of huge importers of fossil fuels to an independent generator and consumer of energy (Ministry of National Infrastructure, Energy and Water Resources). Secondly, it will determine new leases and licenses both for production and exploration respectively. Thirdly, there are massive trade possibilities as Israel becomes a prospective natural gas supplier.

### 3.1.1. Israel's Import History

Israel has a track record of the import of energy for domestic consumption. Before the discovery of its historic gas fields, Israel was principally dependent on the energy import of products such as gas, oil, and coal from different countries in the Eastern Mediterranean. A key supplier of energy to Israel has been Egypt. The import relationship between Israel and Egypt was however short-lived as it lasted only for four years, that's from 2008 to 2012 (Das, 2020). Even though Israel has been a devout importer of natural gas from Egypt, analysts such as Ratner (2011) suggested that it was of vital economic importance for Israel to do away with the natural gas imports from Egypt as it would help Israel improve its balance of trade and provide a greater supply of security.

In 2003, Egypt began exporting gas to Jordan via the 1,200-km-long Arab Gas Pipeline. The pipeline was later stretched to Israel. This latter 100 km-long subsea section connects Ashkelon in Israel to Arish in Egypt. Between 2008 and 2011, Egypt supplied significant amounts of natural gas to Israel howbeit that this supply was prematurely terminated due to insurgencies during the Mubarak regime. It is worth mentioning that Israel, Egypt, and Jordan, both signed a "peace treaty," in the 1970s and 1990s (Hasan, 2020).

Apart from the natural gas supplied to Israel by Egypt, Azerbaijan equally played a great role in supplying energy to Israel. Israel imported significant quantities of crude oil for its domestic consumption. Through the Baku-Tbilisi-Ceyhan pipeline, the crude oil supplied from Azerbaijan passes through Turkey and finally reaches Israel by way of tanker supply (Al-Bayati, 2018).

### 3.1.1.1. Israel's Gas Discoveries: A Louder Voice in the Energy Market

Israel's present status in the energy market is triggered by different gas discoveries made in the past decades. It is well known that Israel has experienced a natural gas evolution which has transformed it from an energy-importing country to a self-sufficient energy producer, consumer, and exporter. The gas discoveries in Israel have revolutionized the gas sector in the country, to the extent that Israel has not only become self-reliant but it is now a major name in the export of natural gas. Since 1999, Israel has seen its upstream industry transformed by the discovery of significant offshore gas fields.

Some of the major gas discoveries in Israel include the Leviathan gas field, Tamar and Tamar SW, Shimshon gas field, Mari B and Nao gas fields, Dalit gas field, Aphrodite/Ishai gas field, and the Karish and Tannin gas fields. These gas fields were of course discovered in different phases and most of them are operated by Noble Energy.

Nobel Energy is an oil and gas company operating onshore in the United States and offshore in the Eastern Mediterranean (Ratner, 2016). The company's headquarters is in Houston, Texas. Examining this company can be beneficial for the understanding of the global economy and politics, as well as the political battle between the winners and losers of the energy transportation. This is based on the fact that Noble Energy has almost owned and controlled the Eastern Mediterranean (EMG) Pipeline.

The first Israeli gas fields, Noa and Mari-B fields were discovered in 1999 and 2000 respectively by Noble Energy. The two fields had joint reserves of over 1.2 tcf (Wood Mackenzie, 2011). Regular gas delivery from the fields as mentioned above began in 2004 and they contributed enormously to Israel's domestic gas consumption even though the reserves are now depleted (Even & Eran, 2014). In 2009, the 9.1 tcf Tamar gas field was discovered by Noble Energy off the coast of Haifa. The Tamar discovery completely changed the gas dynamics of Israel as its reserves were sufficient to furnish its domestic energy for a long time (Wood Mackenzie, 2011).

After the Tamar gas field was discovered, the single most significant discovery in the entire history of Israel was made which was the Leviathan gas field. The Leviathan gas field was discovered in 2010, which is Israel's largest natural gas discovery ever made and has been acknowledged as one of the world's largest natural gas discoveries of the past decade (Wolfrum, 2019).

*3.1.1.2. Israel's Export Option: A Strong Desire to Influence Energy Sector in the Region*
In early 2011, when new natural gas fields were discovered in Israel, it was still unclear whether Israel would become a natural gas exporter. Unabatedly, in recent times, Israel's numerous discoveries of natural gas fields have instigated its demonstration of a strong desire to be readily engaged in the export of natural gas. However, a pertinent question worth analyzing here is, how can Israel develop a sustainable export industry? As it is well known, it is never much of a question if a country wants to export than it is of how that country intends to attain the objective of exportation. Israel, like every other country engaged in the export of any product, is certainly faced with this inherent difficulty. Several studies have been carried out by Israeli experts, where they came up with a handful of options for the exporting of Israeli gas which include (Al-Bayati, 2018):

Firstly, the conversion of the natural gas from the Leviathan gas field into liquefied natural gas (LNG) for export to markets such as Egypt.

The second option was "the construction of a pipeline to Cyprus, connected to a pipeline extending north across the island and then passing down the sea to Turkey, where it could join the pipeline network serving the European market" (Al-Bayati, 2018, p. 25). This option has been analyzed by many scholars including Tsakiris et al. (2018), who asserted that an *Israeli-Cypriot* coalition in the construction of a two-train LNG-export facility as a way of fully utilizing their combined export capacities will stand at 360 bcm for Israel and 110 bcm for Cyprus. According to the above conjecture, a joint *Israel-Cypriot* export facility would have been a golden export opportunity for Israel's newly discovered natural gas, especially in the Leviathan gas fields (as shown in Fig. 2). Such a facility would have been capable of liquefying anywhere between 10 and 14 bcm/y to global markets, especially in Europe (Tsakiris et al., 2018, pp. 4–21).

Furthermore, keeping aside every political string, this option was commercially very logical for two reasons. Firstly, it is "cheaper and faster to create, and it connects Israel to the nearest and largest market" (Al-Bayati, 2018, p. 25). However, the above speculation only ended as a theory as the Israeli government in September 2012, imposed a restriction on the liquefaction of its gas reserves out of Israel.

The failure to strike an initial deal for the construction of an export facility between Israel and Cyprus for the exportation of Israeli natural gas did not in any way frustrate future possibilities of renegotiation between both countries on the very subject. As a matter of fact, in 2017, a bigger possibility surfaced wherein Israel entered into a multilateral agreement with Cyprus, Italy, and Greece. The subject matter of this agreement was the construction of a $6–$7 billion pipeline across the Mediterranean to Europe. Israel's involvement in such a massive project, possibly the longest and deepest sea pipeline in the world, is an outright indication of Israel's ambition to enhance its export potentials in terms of natural gas.

*3.1.1.2.1. Some Major Clawbacks to Israel's Export Possibilities.* The discovery of natural resources seems to be the dream of most countries, but the conversion of such resources from natural resources to a product that is merchandisable is always a heinous task to achieve. This has always been the case with energy-based resources, especially oil and gas. According to Wood Mackenzie (2011), the inability to convert natural gas into a commercial product has a negative effect on exploration and investment. The above and many other speed breaks underlie some of the challenges faced by Israel in relation to its gas sector. One major debate that has been on the table is the preference of the exportation of natural gas at the expense of domestic consumption by the nationals of Israel. Opponents of Israel's gas exportation agenda have argued that the energy needs of Israel should be highly prioritized as it is strategic for Israel's energy autonomy.

This school of thought purport that though Israel's present energy capacity is enormous, they forecast that Israel will suffer from energy shortage and gas reserve depletions by 2030 and onwards. According to Ratner (2011, p. 9),

> A number of factors raise doubts about the viability of exports: Growing domestic demand – and potential new uses for gas, energy security issues, the expense of liquefying the natural gas for transport, an existing global glut of natural gas, and the politics of pipeline exports.

Tsakiris et al. (2018), on their part observe that

> Israel's net export capacity is limited by its own domestic regulations signed in 2013, to 360 bcm, or 40% of its existing proven reserves of almost 900 bcm, then it would need to commit at least

10 bcm/y out of the available 18 bcm/y that it has available for 20 years in order to finance a commercially viable two-train LNG facility in Israel.

## 3.2. The Eastern Mediterranean Pipeline: Source of Tension or Regional Collaboration?

Israel's ambition for the exportation of natural gas is not limited to supplying its neighbors in the East Mediterranean region like Egypt and Jordan. Europe has become a major target market for the export of Israel's gas, and this agenda has been clearly demonstrated by Israel's dire desire for the construction of the Eastern Mediterranean pipeline. The East-Med pipeline is a supposed 1,900-km long and 3-km deep pipeline that will directly connect the Mediterranean gas reserves to mainland Greece through Cyprus (Shaltami, 2020). Approximately 145 km lie in the territorial waters and the EEZ of Israel, and another approximately 600 km of an onshore pipeline in Greece. It will transport natural gas from the Levantine Basin in Israel and from the gas fields in Cypriot waters to Greece and Italy. An approximated sum of about €7 billion is required for the execution of the pipeline within the space of four to five years. The astronomical cost of this project raises issues of profitability (DW, 2020).

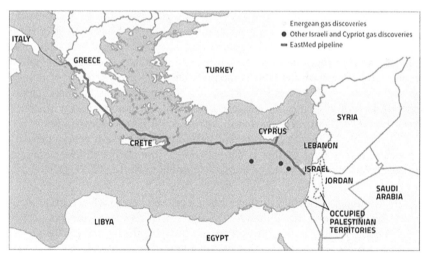

Fig. 2. A 1,900-km Natural Gas Pipeline Project Connects the Eastern Mediterranean's Gas Reserves to Greece and Other European countries. The pipeline cost is approximately €6 billion. On January 2, 2020, the East Med Pipeline accord was signed in Athens by Greece, Cyprus, and Israel leaders. On July 19, 2020, the Israeli government officially approved the accord, allowing the signatory countries to move forward with plans to complete the pipeline by 2025. *Source*: Global Witness (2021).

One may even be tempted to say that if it really worth it to build such an expensive facility for oil exportation, it may be a myopic approach to view the East-Med pipeline project only from the angle of financial returns which will be obtained from the project. Keeping aside the commercial aspirations of the project, it is undeniable that the pipeline will serve a strategic geopolitical interest, mainly of which will be regional integration among the major stakeholders of the Mediterranean region. The pipeline will connect Israel's offshore Leviathan field to Cyprus, continues to Crete island, and ends on the Greek mainland, with the possibility of extending to Italy. It will equally ensure that countries in the Eastern Mediterranean region can control their own foreign policy and security orientation, thereby creating a win-win situation of mutual development and coexistence.

For Israel as a country, the benefits of the East-Med pipeline are far-reaching. The main benefit of the pipeline to Israel is economic advancement than security as purported by some scholars (Wolfrum, 2019).

Apart from the guarantees in economic stability and a strong alliance with the partnering countries, it stands to achieve relative security from the East-Med pipeline (Bassist, 2020). Through the pipeline project, Israel's export potential will be enhanced. The large quantity of natural gas from especially the Leviathan gas field would be easily transported to European markets for sale.

In the tripartite agreement by Israel, Greece, and Cyprus, in July 2020, the Israeli government gave its official approval permitting the signatory countries to move forward with plans to complete the pipeline by 2025 (Shaltami, 2020). This tripartite accord is the first of its kind as it creates the triangular bond between Israel, Greece, and Cyprus, under the auspices of the European Union. The first phase will enhance the transportation of about 10 million bcm of gas annually to Greece and Italy and other south-east European countries. In the second phase, the capacity of the pipeline is expected to rise to a maximum of 20 bcm annually (NS Energy, 2021).

This project has gained huge support from countries like Cyprus, Greece, and Italy, and even from the European Union (EU). The EU has undertaken to fund half the cost of the entire project since it has been considered as a Project of Common Interest (PCI) (Wolfrum, 2019). Turkey on the other hand claims that the pipeline violates its rights which it has over the natural resources found in Cypriot territorial waters. Turkey further contends that the designated route for the pipeline side-lines the long Turkish coastline to deliver gas from the Eastern Mediterranean to Europe. In the words of the Turkish Foreign Minister, the East-Med pipeline is "a new example of futile steps in the region that tries to exclude our country and the Turkish Republic of Northern Cyprus" (Bassist, 2020).

Consequently, Turkey did not stop at allegations but has taken certain strategic steps which could be presumed to be a calculated attempt to frustrate the East-Med pipeline project. In December 2019, Turkey entered into an agreement to create an exclusive economic zone stemming from its southern Mediterranean shore to the northeast coast of Libya. This has prompted reactions and opposition from Israel, Greece, and Cyprus; as the *Turkey-Libyan* exclusive economic zone agenda is deemed to be a stumbling block to the East-Med pipeline project, since the pipeline would have to pass through this exclusive economic zone

(NS Energy, 2021). These moves and Israel's commitment to the East-Med pipeline only stiffen its already strained diplomatic relations with Turkey and wrecks completely any prospect for Israel to ever export its natural gas to Turkey.

In general, these issues are entirely related to the national interests of the superpowers and the key regional players in the eastern Mediterranean, especially Israel, Turkey, and Egypt. Whenever US policy on conflict with Russia and China needs to draw Turkey closer to itself, it will stop supporting the Eastern Mediterranean gas project (because the East-Med gas project bothered Turkey from the beginning), as it did a month before the outbreak of the Ukraine war. The US Embassy in Athens reiterated its commitment to connecting energy in the Eastern Mediterranean to Europe in a statement, indicating that "we are shifting our focus to electricity interconnectors that can support both gas and renewable energy sources." At the same time, whenever the world needs oil and natural gas, the European Union and the United States will try to promote the Eastern Mediterranean Gas Project, describing the East-Med gas project as a strategic alternative to Russian natural gas, as it is visible that only six months after the beginning of the Russo-Ukrainian War, the European Commission President Ursula von der Leyen declared loudly that the "EU seeks to strengthen gas cooperation with Israel in response to Russian blackmail." Thus, on June 15, 2022, the EU signed another agreement with Israel and Egypt to export gas to Europe (DW, 2022).

## 3.3. The Egyptian Gas Market: A Gas Supplier to the European Countries

Egypt is one of Africa's giant gas producers and is ranked 16th in the world in terms of its large oil and gas reserves (BNP Paribas, 2017). According to Tsafos (2015), Egypt's reserves from 1995 to 2010 experienced a geometric increase in its reserves from 22.8 trillion cubic feet (tcf) to 78 tcf. But, that notwithstanding, in recent years, energy consumption in Egypt has plummeted and energy consumers are faced with constant energy shortages. This has pushed Egypt to regress from an energy exporter to an importer (Tsafos, 2015). In line with the recent discoveries of natural gas in Israel and Israel's export options, Egypt has been flagged as a potential market for Israeli natural gas. Ever since this became clear to the world, many questions have come up. Some authors like Hassan (2020) have questioned "why the gas-rich Egypt imports fuel from Israel." Tsafos (2015, p. 1) has also inquired "how did Egypt go from being a booming exporter in the mid-2000s to an importer a decade later."

In an attempt to answer the above questions, a synopsis of Egypt's former energy priorities becomes necessary. As it is well known, Egypt's export history dates far back to the early 2000s during the Hosni Mubarak regime (Hasan, 2020). By 2003, Egypt boasted of markets like Jordan. Egyptian gas was supplied to the Jordanian market through its 1,200-km-long Arab Gas Pipeline which was subsequently extended to Israel. Egypt supplied gas to Israel from 2008 to 2012, but has since encountered 'a sharp macroeconomic deterioration and structural natural resource trends have pushed the sector into difficulties' (Beshay & Devaux, 2017, p. 23). Egypt's supply of gas to the Israeli market though very effective, happened in the short-run.

Israel and Egypt have a long and mixed history characterized by two things – tension and friendship. On the one hand, both countries have been engaged in a series of escalations through wars in the past; while on the other hand, both countries have put their antagonism behind and engaged in peaceful fellowship. A positive outcome of the now peaceful co-existence between both countries is their trade relationship specifically in the domain of energy. Egypt has been a major supplier of Israel's energy needs for some time, though it was short-lived. The Israel–Egypt trade relations in energy have been qualified by some authors as more of a diplomatic than simply a trade and economic relationship (Das, 2020).

It is hard to imagine that Egypt, the world's 12th largest exporter of liquefied natural gas (LNG) in 2022 and 2023, is suffering from an acute domestic fuel shortage. While recurring summer heat waves and a higher demand for cooling are to blame for the crunch, the crisis reflects a deeper problem – a limitation in Egypt's gas production capacity. It raises questions about the country's export potential and has implications for buyers in Europe and elsewhere. Egypt hopes to become a focal point for regional gas trade, facilitating exports of the stranded gas in the Eastern Mediterranean. Compared to its neighbors, Egypt has an established gas transport infrastructure. Israel already sends its gas to Egypt through the Eastern Mediterranean Gas Pipeline (also known as the Arish-Ashkelon pipeline). From there, the commodity can be transported for liquefaction to Egyptian terminals for export (Nakhle, 2023).

The energy crisis in Europe as a result of the Ukraine war increased gas prices dramatically, providing an opportunity for Egypt. LNG exports peaked at 8.9 billion cubic meters in 2022, generating $8.4 billion in revenues compared to $3.5 billion the year before. On the supply side, as depicted in Fig. 3, the situation is rather straightforward: domestic gas production in Egypt has decreased, primarily attributed to a decline in output from the Zohr field (Cousin, 2023).

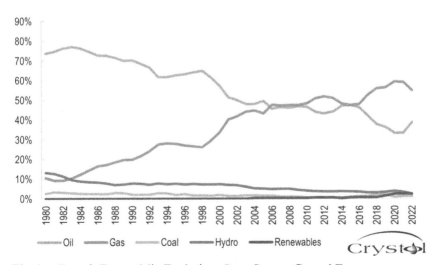

Fig. 3. Egypt's Energy Mix Evolution. *Data Source:* Crystol Energy (Nakhle, 2023).

## 3.4. Cyprus Gas: Position on Sovereignty and Its Market Developments

Since 2010, major gas discoveries have been made in Cyprus, which has helped in reshaping the energy status of Cyprus as a country and its geopolitical position in the Eastern Mediterranean region. It is, however, rather unfortunate that these discoveries were made at the crossroads of a political and economic crisis in Cyprus, coupled with regional squabbles that preceded the Arab Spring and the falling-out of relations between Israel and Turkey.

The exploration activities of Cyprus with regard to the growing natural gas discoveries have indeed sparked up disagreements between the Greek Cypriots on the one hand and the Turkish Cypriots and Turkey on the other. To the Republic of Cyprus, its recent development in natural gas is a golden option to escape the economic crisis it has been facing, and also it has developed into an avenue for the advancement of the national cause against Turkey. It has also paved the way for the creation of better relationships with other countries and multinational companies (Gürel et al., 2013).

In light of the above, exploratory licenses have been granted by Cyprus within its Exclusive Economic Zone (EEZ) and several production sharing contracts (PSC) have been entered into with a couple of global oil and gas companies like Noble Energy. As of now, about eight (08) exploratory licenses have been issued with corresponding PSCs. Consequently, significant exploratory and evaluation work have therefore been carried out by different operators in offshore Cyprus, and the results have been enormous with the discovery of two significant gas fields. The Aphrodite and Glaucus gas fields are the main discoveries made by Noble Energy from 2011 to 2019, which has helped to foster the continuous development of the energy sector of Cyprus (Deloitte Limited, 2018).

In December 2011, the Aphrodite Gas field was discovered by Noble Energy with the capacity of approximately 5 to 8 trillion cubic feet (tcf) of natural gas, which is equivalent to 141 to 226 billion cubic meters (bcm) of gas (Lakes, 2012). However, the existing energy demand in Cyprus is less than 1 bcm per year. The gas in the Aphrodite field is therefore more than sufficient to electrify Cyprus for a century (Gürel et al., 2013). While the Aphrodite brought in better prospects to the Cypriot energy sector; it has on the other hand bred economic conflicts, including rights to participation in the exploitation of the natural gas discovered in the Exclusive Economic Zone (EEZ) of Cyprus. In clearer terms, "the high expectations created with the discovery of natural gas fields in the Eastern Mediterranean region are directly affecting the behaviour of the political actors involved in the Cypriot conflict" (Palacios, 2018, p. 11).

Turkey and Greece are political stakeholders in Cyprus, and their political agenda concerns the gas discoveries in Cyprus. The presence of these two countries (as a keen state's role) and called motherland has only made the sovereignty problem in Cyprus more visible and has impeded the peace settlement in Cyprus. This however is contrary to popular opinion which was to the effect that the natural gas resources discovered in this region would have served as a motivation for peace settlement, eradicating hostilities between the two Cypriot communities.

While tensions escalated in Cyprus after the 2011 gas discovery, the issue is inherently linked to the long historical disputes over national sovereignty.

### 3.4.1. Sovereignty Versus Equality: Some Ramifications of the Cypriot Natural Gas Sector

For decades, sovereignty has been the key problem underlying the political and economic landscape of Cyprus. The former British colony at the time of its independence was made up of two factions that are the Greek Cypriots and the Turkish Cypriots. Owing to the fact that the two major factions of Cyprus had historical affiliations to two sovereign states, which are Greece and Turkey, they therefore became natural stakeholders over Cyprus and key parties to the agreements that culminated to its independence. These agreements included the Zurich-London Agreements of 1959, the Treaties of Guarantee and Alliance, the Treaty on the Establishment of the RoC, and the Republic of Cyprus (RoC) Constitution. All these agreements were signed between the UK on the one hand, as the colonial master, then Greece and Turkey on the other hand as stakeholders.

In the constitution of Cyrus, it was agreed upon for the RoC to take the status of a bi-communal state in which both communities – the Greek and the Turkish Cypriots were to have partial communal autonomy and share power between them. Also, equal treatment in terms of their participation in the state organs was a very important provision of the constitution (Gürel et al., 2013).

The rationale for the provisions stemmed from the fact that Turkish Cypriots constituted the minority while Greek Cypriots were the majority, and as such it was intended to strike an equilibrium in power between the two communities. However, in 1964, Turkish Cyprus withdrew from the RoC and later on formed what is known as the Turkish Republic of Northern Cyprus (TRNC). With the separation of these two communities, governance remained in the hands of the Greek Cypriot community, and consequently, as time went on, Greek Cyprus acquired international recognition as the legitimate authority of the RoC with the complicity of the UN Security Council.

Meanwhile, the Greek Cypriots have since governed the RoC, the Turkish Cypriots have governed their own now-called TRNC. Attempts have been made since 1968 to resolve the Cyprus problem to no avail, and every effort to reunify them has proven futile. Since their separation, there has not been any concession between the Greek and Turkish Cyprus on the partitioning of their collective possessions or resources. As a matter of fact, the discovery of natural resources in recent times in the maritime regions of Cyprus and its exploitation by just one part of the divide has been the reason for recent escalations between the Greek and the Turkish Cyprus.

Evidently, this has only increased more the battle for sovereignty and the debate on the equitable sharing of the natural resources. While Turkish Cyprus on the one hand has made demands for their fair share of the natural gas discoveries made in Cyprus within the last decade, Greek Cypriots or what is formally called the RoC, have maintained complete sovereignty and exclusive rights over every natural resource found on the territory of Cyprus (Olgun, 2019). In as much as the Greek Cyprus is the internationally recognized community over the RoC, their decision to exclude Turkish Cypriots from participating in the partitioning of the natural resources has come under scrutiny and international condemnation. The UN Secretary General, Antonio Guterres, during his 2018 visit to Cyprus, insisted in strong terms that both Greek and Turkish Cyprus have rights over the natural resources discovered in Cyprus (UN Security Council, 2019).

Mustafa E. Olgun, (2019) has termed it a violation of the international legal framework which created and bound the two states during the time of the independence of Cyprus. The International Crisis Group (2012) affirms the sovereign right of the RoC to exploit the resources in its maritime region but however, they have pointed out that the fact that the Greek Cypriots went about with the exploration of those natural resources singlehandedly is a violation of the agreements to share natural resources between the former two-communities.

The Treaty of Guarantee is instrumental to the problem of sovereignty in present day Cyprus. According to this treaty,

> Under the Treaty of Guarantee; Greece, Turkey, and the UK recognize and guarantee the independence, territorial integrity and security of the Republic of Cyprus, and also the state of affairs established by the Basic Articles of its Constitution. In the event of a breach, the three guarantor countries were afforded the right to take action – jointly or, if that proved impossible, individually – for the restoration of the guaranteed regime. (Gürel et al., 2013, pp. 31–32)

### 3.4.2. Aphrodite Gas Field: A Gift or a Curse?

Ten years ago, when the Aphrodite gas field was discovered in Block 12 of the exclusive economic zone of Cyprus, expectations were very high for both domestic consumption and exportation prospects. It was expected that the development of Cypriot natural gas reservoirs would bring along certain benefits including revolutionizing of the energy sector of Cyprus, providing it with strong energy independence and high exportation capacity. It was also expected that it would be an instrument for the re-stratification of the geopolitical status of Cyprus as well as its relationship with other states in the Eastern Mediterranean region. But as it is well known, the Aphrodite discovery has ignited disputes between the RoC and the TRNC ownership and participation in the proceeds of the natural gas discoveries.

After the Aphrodite gas field was discovered in 2011 in the RoC, the Greek Cypriots single-handedly commenced drilling without the acknowledgment of the Turkish Cypriots which prompted heavy disapproval from Turkey. For the purpose of clarity, it is important to state that the conflict in Cyprus is not merely a resultant effect of the Aphrodite gas discovery, but a result of debates as to who has rights over the marked-out areas where natural gas was discovered. The International Crisis Group (2012) brings in another element which has contributed to the current dispute in Cyprus. They assert that in as much as the "contested maritime boundaries and exploration of natural gas deposits off the divided island are the sources of the current dispute, but tensions also result from the slowdown of UN-mediated Cyprus reunification talks" (International Crisis Group, 2012, p. 1).

Turkey has refused to recognize the RoC as a sovereign state and therefore challenges its right to enter into EEZ contracts or to unilaterally enjoy any exploratory rights over the territory without an inclusive settlement. Turkey alleges that the RoC which is predominantly a Greek Cypriot regime lacks the territorial competence over the entire territory since it does not represent the interests of Turkish Cypriots (Kumar, 2020).

From the foregoing, it is evident that the presence of the Aphrodite gas field has rather increased the gap between the once two brotherly states, to a disposition of constant debates over sovereignty and rights of exploration of energy found on the territory of Cyprus. A new approach is therefore needed for amicable discussion on collective rights of exploration as well as sharing of the proceeds from energy emanating from Cyprus.

### 3.4.3. *Exploration and Market Trends in the Cypriot Gas Sector*

Since the discovery of the Aphrodite gas field, there has been a lengthy delay in the development especially due to doubts over the commercialization of the natural gas and conceding on production share agreements. Before the discovery of the Aphrodite, the Greek Administration of Southern Cyprus (GASC) had granted exploration rights to companies with a price attached to those rights. In October 2008, the GASC conceded with Noble Energy giving Noble the complete gas exploration rights over Block 12 on which the Aphrodite gas field was discovered. This concession was tied to a Production Sharing Agreement (PSA) between the GASC government and Noble Energy. The terms of the PSA shifted the burden of providing capital, technology, and staff to the contractors (Taneri et al., 2019). The PSA over the Aphrodite field was 60:40 for the government and Noble Energy respectively.

In 2015, the Aphrodite gas field was declared commercially viable by its developers and export options were already being considered. Egypt was as of 2015 flagged as the target market for the exportation of Cypriot natural gas. However, in 2016 such options came to nothing due to the huge cost entailed in building an LNG facility by Cyprus. That notwithstanding, in 2018, agreements were made between Cyprus and Egypt for the exportation of natural gas to Egypt. Even though this initiative was hamstringed by the outbreak of COVID-19, better options presented themselves to Cyprus like the Mediterranean pipeline project. With the above project, other market options like Cyprus selling its natural gas to the European market become a new trend in the market options of Cyprus. In 2015, Cyprus amidst Greece and Italy acknowledged the East Mediterranean Project (Ellinas, 2016).

Finally, in January 2020, Greece and Cyprus signed the final agreement for the pipeline project alongside Greece and Israel. It will provide an opportunity for Cyprus to merge with the European gas system, which will further enhance gas trading in the south-east European region. East Mediterranean tough operations are only expected to start in 2025 and will foster the economic development of Cyprus by providing a stable market for gas exports.

## 3.5. Egypt and Trilateral Partnerships

Gas exploration and production have been a major part of the Egyptian economy since the 1960s (Okumuş, 2020). After Algeria, Egypt is the second largest gas producer in Africa (Tsakiris, 2018). Energy discoveries as it is well known, are always a natural wealth generator, but has its downsides as they always come with a mixed blessing of either conflict or cooperation. Egypt as a repository of natural gas has suffered both fates. In a bid to reconcile its positions, Egypt strives to come out with new ways and possibilities to make the most of its security and make certain its survival, and at the same time still determined to impart its own agenda to the Eastern Mediterranean geopolitical order. Egypt has therefore entered into different partnerships, with neighboring countries of the Eastern Mediterranean region for different reasons which will be examined below.

### 3.5.1. The Egyptian, Greek, and Cypriot Triangle

In 2014, Egypt started preparing the grounds for a trilateral relationship between itself, Greece, and Cyprus. This new partnership was designed to create a cordial economic and political relationship with Greece and Cyprus, and to unleash the full potential of the Eastern Mediterranean region for the benefit of the three countries and also for the entire region. While the alliance is for the general interests of the three countries, it has great significance to Egypt as it will enable Egypt to uphold its strategic interests in the unexplored waters of the conflict-rich Mediterranean region (Shama, 2019).

In September 2014, these three countries met in Cairo for the Egypt-Greece-Cyprus Trilateral Summit where they came up with the Cairo Declaration. Amongst other things, the Cairo Declaration affirmed the collective need for the three countries to tackle the major challenges faced in the Eastern Mediterranean region, such as instability and security upheavals (Ministry of Foreign Affairs of the Hellenic Republic, 2014). The consolidation of this relationship has been further reaffirmed by establishing an annual tripartite summit. Another angle of their cooperation is in the field of oil and gas. In the last summit of October 2020, tripartite nations expressed the desire to enhance continuity in their cooperation in relation to the various exploration and gas transfer agreements, which further highlights the fact that the discovery of hydrocarbon reserves can serve as a catalyst for regional stability and prosperity (Gavriella, 2020).

From an Egyptian standpoint, what is the motivation underlying the cultivation of close ties with Cyprus and Greece? What are the nature, the potential, and the limitations of the tripartite alliance? And to what extent can this political alignment alter the balance of power and the security architecture in the Eastern Mediterranean and the wider Middle East?

### 3.5.2. Egypt–Israel Gas Export Partnership

The Egyptian–Israeli relationship has been a long and antagonistic one since the bible days. In modern days, the two countries have had several confrontations like the wars fought in 1948, 1956, 1967, 1969, 1970, and 1973. However, these confrontations came to an end in 1979 with the signing of a peace agreement between Egypt and Israel known as the Camp David Accords (Das, 2020).

Ever since, there have been robust efforts by both countries to foster cooperation between them. One pragmatic way that both countries have adopted in furthering their relationship has been to enter into energy supply agreements. As it is well known, Israel is at the moment a significant supplier of natural gas to Egypt. But before the historic natural gas discoveries were made in Israel, Egypt was a major gas supplier to Israel. To this end, two lines of partnerships will be considered under this sub-topic, that is the Egypt–Israeli partnership where Egypt was the supplier on the one hand, and on the other, the Israeli–Egypt partnership where Israel is the supplier.

### 3.5.3. Egypt–Israeli Gas Supply and Purchase Agreement

In 2005, Egypt and Israel signed a gas supply and purchase agreement wherein Egypt was to supply gas to Israel for a period of 20 years. This agreement was however short-lived as it was discontinued barely four years after it commenced. Gas exportation from Egypt to Israel started in 2008, and in 2011 it was prematurely and singlehandedly terminated by Egypt during the Mubarak regime (Hasan, 2020).

This move has indeed put the relationship between both countries on a scale balance and has caused a stalemate in bilateral ties between them. Meanwhile, major stakeholders like the Eastern Mediterranean Gas (EMG) have concluded that Egypt's decision was made in bad faith and highly unlawful, it still remains an even bigger debate if Egypt's move was a political decision. Das (2020) in his argument, has pinned his analysis around the political events which unfolded in Egyptian political landscape around the time of Egypt's breach. According to him, Egypt had come under persistent rebuke about its ties with Israel during the Arab Spring in 2011. He further explains that it was during the period of political transition in Egypt where the supply of gas to Israel was disrupted due to several insurgencies and bombing of pipelines. Contrary to the above argument, statesmen of both countries have debunked such debates by reaffirming to themselves and the world that the discontinuance of gas supply by Egypt to Israel was strictly a commercial decision. Benjamin Netanyahu, Israeli Prime Minister has reiterated that the termination was strictly business-related and void of politics (Ahren, 2012).

In 2012, Egypt and Israel entered into a 15-year contract for Israel's exportation of 85 billion cubic meters (bcm) of natural gas, from Israeli offshore gas fields – Leviathan and Tamar. From all indications, the Israeli–Egypt gas export agreement will help to create a mechanism for long-term regional cooperation based on common interests (Yellinek, 2020). Through the agreement, the Egyptian company, Dophinus Holdings will buy from Israel. On the 9th of January 2019, Israel exported the first consignment of gas to Egypt.

### 3.5.4. Egypt and Turkey: Continued Tensions or Common Ground for Rapprochement?

Egypt and Turkey for a long time have had a tense and competitive relationship. Their bonds fell put in 2013 after the Egyptian military overthrew Muslim Brotherhood President Mohammed Morsi who was a great ally of the Turkish President Erdoğan. Maritime boundaries have also contributed a great deal to their scuffles (Reuters, 2021). As Egypt moves to energy self-sufficiency, it has entered into more and more exploration and production agreements with foreign companies which Turkey has criticized as an attempt by Egypt to put Turkey in direct competition with foreign companies (Al-Monitor, 2020).

Meanwhile, there is a growing need for both countries to mend up bilateral ties; the possibility of them reaching any agreement as of now remains a theory. Recently, there has been growing speculation that Turkey may open talks with Egypt on maritime demarcation with Egypt. Mevlüt Çavuşoğlu, Turkey's foreign affairs minister, has recently stated that "As the two countries with the longest coastlines in the eastern Mediterranean, if our ties and the conditions allow it, we can also negotiate a maritime demarcation deal with Egypt and sign it among ourselves" (Aksoy, 2021).

## 3.6. Turkey and Its Geo-Strategic Vision Toward Natural Gas in the Eastern Mediterranean and Europe

Since 2010, natural gas and oil have been discovered in the Eastern Mediterranean, and substantial multinational energy companies have flocked to the region alongside Turkey for over two decades. The hydrocarbon issue has directly impacted regional negotiations. Large gas field discoveries in the region have prompted the massive exploration, production, and commercialization of natural gas. While the recent gas trends have fueled a mixed feeling of cooperation and conflict, Turkey's geographical location sets it in a pivotal position, which helps the country play a vital role and goes a long way toward influencing its geopolitical agenda in terms of the natural gas in the Eastern Mediterranean region.

> Turkey's unique geopolitical situation derives from the fact that it is poor in hydrocarbon reserves while its neighborhood has abundant resources. This provides an imperative for Ankara to pursue stable energy ties with energy-rich countries or regions in its proximity. (Kozma, 2020)

Turkey is strategically positioned between two different continents that are partly in Asia and in Europe. It lies at the junction of the Balkans, Caucasus, Middle East, and the eastern Mediterranean (Dewdney, 2021). Because of its strategic positioning, becoming an international physical hub and transit corridor for natural gas is at the top of Turkey's energy vision. Turkey targets at consolidating its position as a transit route of natural gas from the Eastern Mediterranean region (Tsakiris et al., 2018).

Apart from serving as a passage for natural gas, Turkey's desire for exploration of natural gas has increased recently as the country strives to achieve energy independence. Also, Turkey wants a buyout from its immense budgetary deficit situation caused by the persistent import of energy. It is well known that Turkey's domestic energy needs are satisfied through massive gas importation from other countries. According to Dalay (2021),

> through hydrocarbon exploration, Turkey hopes to address its chronic economic problems. To this end, the country has doubled down on its energy exploration activities both in the Eastern Mediterranean and the Black Sea, which recently culminated in a major gas discovery. (p. 3)

Amidst Turkey's quest to the top, its relationship with other countries in the Eastern Mediterranean region has not been a cordial one. Turkey has been absent from the major efforts of regional cooperation. It is therefore important to question how Turkey intends to achieve its objectives with its antagonistic relationship with major stakeholders in the region. In 2014, Turkey–Egypt relationships failed following the overthrow of Egypt's President Mohammed Morsi. Recently, Egypt's engagement with five different foreign companies for the exploration of gas has been highly condemned by Turkey and seen as a calculated attempt to open Turkey to foreign competitors.

Turkey has great opportunities for alliance in the region, such as the Eastern Mediterranean pipeline project which it is interested in, and also the Eastern Mediterranean Gas Forum (EMGF). The EMGF is a recent regional effort to foster cooperation between the countries in the Eastern Mediterranean region and Turkey's absence from such an initiative leaves more to be desired (Kozma, 2020).

It therefore begs for the question of how Turkey intends to achieve its vision with its isolationist principle. As it has been stated above, Turkey's deficiency of gas reserves is a perfect reason why it should cooperate with energy-rich countries in the region. The best way for Turkey to achieve its geo-strategic vision in terms of natural gas is to reconsider cooperation and alliance with the major energy E&P countries in the region.

Over a decade now, the massive discovery of hydrocarbons in the Eastern Mediterranean region, specifically in Israel, Cyprus, and Egypt has made the region a center for international energy talks (European Parliament, 2017). Apart from gaining energy independence and the satisfaction of domestic demands, the exportation of hydrocarbons to both regional and international markets has been a major characteristic of this new energy dawn in the Eastern Mediterranean. Accordingly, Europe has become a major market and a huge importer of the Eastern Mediterranean gas, and as such a multidimensional European–Mediterranean partnership has been established. Though the domestic gas consumption in Europe has always risen and fallen, the aggregate consumption is always high.

To this effect, the European Energy Security Strategy has focused on the significance of gas, stressing the need to diversify the sources of gas deliveries, increase LNG imports, and develop local shale gas production (Winrow, 2016). While Russia, Norway, Algeria, and the Netherlands have been the major exporters of natural gas to Europe, the need for diversification of their import hubs has become more important to Europe. Also, the use of other "dirtier" fossil fuels like coal and oil keeps getting unpopular by the day and the quest to transition to gas is now stronger in Europe than ever.

Gas from the Eastern Mediterranean region has therefore become the next best alternative for the European gas importation. The big Eastern Mediterranean gas players like Israel, Cyprus, and Egypt who were importers turned exporters, have swiftly engaged in a full export option into the European gas market.

Theodoros Tsakiris (2018, p. 37) has reiterated the importance of the Eastern Mediterranean gas to Europe by indicating that "the East-Med can provide new sources of gas to the EU, thereby helping the Union meet its strategic objective of limiting its increasing dependence on Gazprom." He further opines that the Eastern Mediterranean gas "could emerge as a new source of indigenous supply that could partly compensate for the rapid decline of domestic EU production in the North Sea" (Tsakiris, 2018, p. 37). According to the EU Commission Quarterly Report on the European gas markets, in 2019, European indigenous gas production plummeted by 9% which is an approximation of 2.6 bcm. It further reveals that the UK, Netherlands, and Romania which are the biggest gas producers in Europe suffered from a decline in their production (EU Commission Quarterly Report, 2019).

## 3.7. Israeli–Europe Gas Trade

As of 2013, Israel's export options were well defined, by rationing its reserves into a 60:40 ratios, keeping 60% for home consumption, and 40% for regional and international markets. The 40% reserved for regional and international markets could be estimated to approximately 360 bcm. Though this was a good export capacity, at the time, it was very burdensome to Israel to realize its export potential due to the absence of sponsors at the time that could facilitate the construction of export facilities. However, this problem has recently been solved with the 1,900-km long and 3-km deep pipeline Eastern Mediterranean pipeline project which will be the longest and deepest gas transportation facility in the world. This pipeline facility is a giant step in the realization of the export options of Israel and other stakeholders like Cyprus and Egypt.

The fact that about half of the 7 billion Euros required by the project will be sponsored by the European Union is only an added advantage for Israel as a nation and other stakeholders like Egypt and Cyprus (Tsakiris, 2018). This also is a clear indication of how important the Eastern Mediterranean gas is to the European Energy Security.

## 3.8. Egypt–European Gas Trade

Though many have questioned whether Egypt has what it takes to be a major hub for gas exportation, Egypt continues to aim high at becoming a major hub for the exportation of LNG to Europe. Egypt's gas statistics from 2015 however proves to be very promising and actually makes the possibility of it becoming a gas hub and exporter to Europe very likely. In 2015, Egypt's discovery of the Zohr Gas field changed the narrative and catapulted it to becoming the world's 16th largest gas reserve holder with an approximated reserve capacity of 65 trillion cubic feet (tcf). By 2018, Egypt's reserve increased geometrically to 75.5 tcf (BP Statistical Review of World Energy, 2019). Over time, by December 2020, Egypt's production skyrocketed to approximately 6.6 billion cubic feet per day. It was forecasted that by 2021, Egypt's natural gas production capacity production would be 7.2 billion cubic feet of natural gas per day (Reuters, 2021).

Egypt has since the Zohr discovery engaged in exporting its natural gas to foreign markets including Europe and Asia. According to the BP Statistical Review of World Energy (2019), Egypt's export of LNG has been on a constant rise since 2016. In 2016, there were 0.8 billion cubic meters (Cub) of LNG; 1.2 Cub in 2017, and 2.0 in 2018. Of all the exports of 2018, about 1.1 Cub were exported to Norway and other European countries. By 2019, the export rate doubled to 4.5 Cub (Egypt Today, 2019). Even though Egypt's export rate in 2019 increased to 4.5 Cub, Egypt did not record any export of TNG to any market including Europe. Recent trends in 2020 cast doubt if Egypt is up to the task of becoming a major gas exporter. In 2020, natural gas exports plummeted from 4.5 to 1.8 Cub and there were no trade movements in the form of LNG (Statistical Review of World Energy, 2021).

## 3.9. Cypriot–European Gas Trade

In the last decade, Cyprus has made two significant natural gas discoveries – the Aphrodite and Glaucus gas fields. The Aphrodite with a 7 trillion tcf capacity and the Glaucus with a 5–8 tcf, Cyprus has demonstrated great prospects for export to both regional and international markets like Europe. The 2019 ExxonMobil Glaucus discovery is said to be the third-largest natural gas field discovered in the world (Geo Expro, 2019), which of course has a huge impact in the export options of Cyprus. In 2019, Cyprus concluded an agreement with Israel and Egypt for the construction of the Eastern Mediterranean pipeline which will aid in the transportation of LNG from their respective countries to the market in Europe.

The prospects for gas export by Cyprus have not been a straight one. It has been faced with both regulatory and political issues. Firstly, even though Cyprus now boasts of large gas reserves, its domestic energy needs will play a huge role in the quantity of gas which will be earmarked for export. In 2013, it was projected by the Cyprus Energy Regulatory Authority (CERA) that domestic consumption would be approximately 25 bcm by 2035. The implication of the above projection has a huge impact on the export options of Cyprus as the quantity of gas open for export shrinks from 198 bcm to 173 bcm (Gürel et al., 2013).

Also, there are a handful of contingencies which stand a hindrance to the achievement of the Cypriot export agenda. Since the separation between the Republic of Cyprus and the Turkish Republic of Northern Cyprus, there have been political disputes between the Greek and Turkish Cypriots over sovereignty and energy rights. This dispute has prompted Turkey's intervention in it to support the interests of the Turkish Cypriots. There was a very long delay in the exploration of the Aphrodite field due to some negotiation hurdles.

## 3.10. The Syrian Crisis within the New Geopolitical Change in the Mediterranean

Syria, positioned on the east coast of the Mediterranean Sea in the South Western Asia and in the north of the Arabian Peninsula in the Middle East, is a country with a strategic geographic importance (Hilali, 2016). Since 2011, Syria has been undergoing a civil war which of course has not only affected its internal affairs but also has an overwhelming effect on the entire Middle Eastern and the Eastern Mediterranean region as a whole (Delanoë, 2014). When the Syrians began what can be termed as a peaceful anti-government protest in 2011, the slightest possibility of the outbreak of a civil war was inconceivable. The crisis degenerated from one stage to another, and it transcended the nation of Syria to the involvement of non-state actors from far and near (Tan & Perudin, 2019).

While the Syrian crisis portrays itself as a mere political shakedown, multiple authors have suggested the presence of ulterior influences to be the fuel behind the Syrian crisis and the reason behind its persistence.

According to Mirza et al. (2021), the lifespan of the Syrian crisis has witnessed a proliferation of the interference of non-state actors due to their high affinity for oil. Therefore, they inquire as to the hidden agenda which propelled the crisis to metamorphose from an internal affair to an international affair. According to this, they assert that conflicts of interest by the various non-state interveners among others are the main factor that has led to the disintegration of the once-known peaceful anti-government demonstrations to what has now turned into a full-blown civil war. In the same line, some authors have pinpointed that behind the Syrian crisis is the race for energy dominance.

Delanoë (2014, p. 4) argues that

> the Syrian crisis has been fuelled by energy competition between several actors: Qatar and Iran, Turkey which aims at becoming an energy hub between the East and West, and Russia which seeks to maintain its monopoly on the gas supply to Europe.

As it is well known, the Middle Eastern states are repositories of approximately 41% of the world's natural gas reserves; Iran and Qatar own approximately 31.6 out of the 41% (Karim, 2016). As Karim (2016, p. 111) has argued,

> most of the regional and foreign belligerents in the Syrian war are gas exporting countries with interests in one of the two competing pipeline projects that seeks to cross Syrian territory to deliver either Qatari or Iranian gas to Europe.

Countries like the United States, Russia, Turkey, Iran, Iraq, Jordan, Israel, and Saudi Arabia have played diverse roles in the crisis. While Russia and Iran pledged their full support to the Assad regime, the United States, Turkey, Saudi Arabia, and many other Arab nations have sided with opposition forces (Mirza et al., 2021).

The United States on its part has given ceaseless support to the opposition, the Syrian Democratic Forces (SDF) in the quest to see a change of government. In this respect, certain measures have been taken to ensure its realization. In August 2011, the United States gave an economic sanction against Syria by virtue of an executive order No 13582, restricting the US export or sale of services to Syria, barring the import of Syrian petroleum or Syrian petroleum products, and prohibiting the US citizens from participating in any deal concerning the petroleum products from Syria (Administration of Barack Obama, 2011).

### 3.10.1. Syrian Oil and Gas: How Did It Influence the Syrian Crisis?

Syria is generally known to be a minor producer of oil and gas as compared to the major producers in the Mediterranean region (Knell, 2013). It has an approximated oil reserve of about 2.6 billion barrels; which had prior to the broke out of the 2011 crisis witnessed a steep decline to a production level of below 400,000 bpd before 2011. Syria is ranked 31st in the world in terms of oil reserves, 70th in terms of production, and 68th in terms of consumption (Worldometer, 2016).

The oil from Syria is said to be one of the cheapest, most of which is exported (Shaban, 2019). Talking about gas, Syria is ranked 42nd, 53rd, and 63rd in the world in terms of natural gas reserves, global gas production, and consumption respectively.

Even though Syria's role in the global production of oil is minor, its geographical position has a vital geopolitical status as a potential energy transit hub. Worth noting is the fact that Syria is bordered by Turkey in the north, Lebanon and Israel in the southwest, Iraq in the east and southeast, and Jordan in the south which of course gives it a strategic importance in the region (Hilali, 2016). Syria is linked by pipeline to Egypt, Jordan, Lebanon, and Iraq. Because of the Syrian crisis since 2011, many of these pipeline projects have come to a halt. Experts argue that regional competition for access to pipeline routes and international energy markets is a major factor driving the non-state actors' involvement in the Syrian conflict (The Syrian Report, 2021).

According to Shaban (2019), Russia's support prompted the Assad regime's full intervention into Syria, leading to what it is now seen to be the Russian dominance and control over Syria. This action of control over Syria has far-reaching implications on Syria's position as a route for oil and gas transmission. Shaban (2019, p. 3) has further stated that

> Controlling Syria's territory means blocking any attempt to establish a natural gas pipeline from the Middle East towards Europe. Given Russia's role in Libya, it seems that Russia is trying to tighten the ring around Europe to make it one day at the mercy of only Russian gas.

The Syria Report (2021) holds that the oil and gas sector in Syria suffered greatly during the war, with constant destruction of energy infrastructures like pipelines, and also from international plunder and smuggling of oil and gas. According to BBC, the government of Syria has accused the United States of oil theft from Syria. Russia which is a key ally to President Assad corroborated the allegations by describing the act of the United States as "international state banditry." This allegation came after the then US president has indicated that the United States should benefit from Syrian oil (Reality Check Team, 2019).

In line with the previous arguments, the geopolitical position of Syria and its strategic route for oil and gas transmission by major players in the race of energy have contributed enormously in the degeneration of the Syrian crisis from a peaceful protest to a full-blown war.

While it seems as though non-state actors' intervention is for human rights and humanitarian purposes, existing data indicates that the above are only secondary reasons while the major reason remains as dominance in the race of oil and gas. That is to say, the presence of abundant oil in the region is one of the factors that have triggered the warring parties.

Chapter Four

# Oil and Gas in the Iraqi Kurdistan: Geopolitical Connectivity and the Market Realities

## Abstract

The Kurdistan Region of Iraq (KRI) stands as a significant player in the hydrocarbon landscape of the Middle East, necessitating an in-depth analysis of its role in the exportation process to Turkey and Mediterranean ports, thereby fostering economic and political ties and projecting toward the future. Situated as a semi-autonomous entity in northern Iraq, the Kurdistan Region boasts abundant natural gas resources, attracting interest from Russian firms and Turkish stakeholders. However, Iran's influence in Iraq and the wider region poses a regional threat to the Kurdistan Region's natural resources. This chapter meticulously examines the oil and gas blocks within the Kurdistan Region amidst the backdrop of transformative global energy market shifts, including the impacts of the COVID-19 pandemic and the Russian–Ukrainian conflict. Through this lens, it seeks to delineate the Kurdistan Region's political and economic positioning within the evolving regional order.

*Keywords*: Kurdistan Region of Iraq (KRI); natural resources; Ceyhan Port; Iraq-Turkey Pipeline (ITP); Kurdistan Pipeline

## 4.1. An Overview of the De-facto Kurdistan Region – Iraq

The Middle East and the Eastern Mediterranean have gained more strategic importance from the Western point of view. This is because it is located between the three continents of Asia, Europe, and Africa. The Middle East also plays a vital role in providing oil and natural gas and maintaining the balance in the global energy market.

Hence, the Kurdistan Region of Iraq, which has been bolstered as one of the sub-unit players in the hydrocarbon of the Middle East region, is required to be analyzed through the exporting process from Iraq and the Kurdistan Region to Turkey and the Mediterranean ports, building thus economic and political bridges and connecting them with the future. As well as political economy, better known as political processes, is an appropriate and more explicable approach to understanding how politics affect the economic outcomes of the Kurdistan Region of Iraq (KRI). To a greater extent, this terminology incarnates the idea that economics is not separable from politics *stricto sensu*. The underlying widespread view emanates from the belief that political factors are at the center of determining economic outcomes. Hence, economics as a discipline also significantly influences the forces of every political system (Sorenson, 2010).

Although Kurds are without their autonomous nation-state, one can say without any fear of contradiction that Kurds remain the largest ethnic group territorially concentrated in the Middle East. However, the population of the Kurdish Region of Iraq seems to be different since it has been striving to create its managerial trajectory to establish an independent political order for more than a century. The net effect of this action is that the Kurdish region in the north of Iraq is a high-ranking candidate when speculating about forming several new states in the Middle East. The visible events since Baghdad have lesser influence in the region; given that the Iraqi Kurds have established and empowered a government of their own, administration, armed forces, and a parliament that is independently pursuing their policies contrary to the will of their parent state (Jüde, 2017).

Kurdistan remains a semi-autonomous region of Iraq, with a proven 45 billion barrels of oil and a natural gas reserve of 200 trillion cubic feet (5.7 trillion cubic meters). This economic strength in terms of natural resources has motivated and triggered other states along the Mediterranean and Europe to rush into the formation of economic relationships (Ismael, 2018). "During the Atlantic Council's Global Energy Forum in Dubai in March 2022, the Prime Minister of the Kurdistan Regional Government Masrour Barzani announced that 'We will become a net export of natural gas to Iraq, Turkey and Europe soon'" (Daily Sabah, 2022).

To this effect, a Kurdish–Turkish energy relationship exists between Europe and Russia. How have the natural resources of the KRI mentioned above acted as a motivation to the Eastern Mediterranean bloc? The KRI's energy capacity has the potential to transform geopolitics significantly. However, political divisions and ongoing disputes have complicated the process of realizing this possibility. Baghdad has also traditionally leveraged its energy sector control to secure concessions in political disputes critical to the Kurdistan Regional Government's (KRG) existence. Nevertheless, both Iraq and Iran realize that Iran's gas supplies are insufficient for Iraq's energy needs, which heightens the importance of Kurdish gas reserves and raises the imperative of a compromise (Alaaldin, 2023). The presence of the Kurdistan Region in the regional chessboard is required, like asking How can the Kurdistan Region demonstrate its willingness to form a strategic triangle with Gulf Corporation Council and Turkey?

This chapter also aims to inspect the KRI's oil and gas industry to determine its actual condition. Moreover, the study offers a new idea to see the KRI's hydrocarbon resources as a common ground in world affairs as Realists and neo-realists focus on the readiness of powerful countries as unitary players. Therefore, all actions can only uphold oil and natural gas when the powerful states push them. Threats on oil and gas resources, water resources, renewable energy, and electrification, for example, are assumed to be oriented and promoted by the most powerful states to administer some form of order in international systems. Therefore, the Kurdistan Region likely needs to be a part of the new regional and global order to maintain its energy security and promote the Kurdish entity. Consequently, this study recommends procedures that may help avoid disappointing outcomes for the KRI's oil and gas industry.

The global shifts following the Cold War and the unprecedented failure of Saddam's regime during the 1991 Second Gulf War were pivotal in the emergence of the KRG. In those tumultuous times, the oppressive actions of the Baath regime led to a surge in refugees, primarily Kurds, capturing the attention of international players such as the United Nations, the United States, France, and Britain. Responding to this crisis, the United Nations intervened with Resolution 688 of the Security Council. Meanwhile, the United States, Britain, and France took action, implementing no-fly zones over the northern region of Iraq and exerting influence over the rest of the country. This intervention involved approximately 225,000 flights between 1991 and 2003, with France withdrawing from the effort in 1996 (Rogg & Rimscha, 2007).

The perpetual fighting between the Kurds and Iraqi forces did not stop until October 1991, when the Iraqi forces eventually left the Kurdish region. The region assumed an independent status, and after that, proclaimed a de facto autonomous power with the formation of a Kurdish Regional Government and a regional parliament in 1992. Therefore, the Kurdistan Region of Iraq is the territory located on the northeastern border of Iraq. Moreover, legally known today as a federal region as per the 2005 constitution of Iraq, the region is one of its kind, given that it is multi-ethnic and multi-religious, which is an attribute that distinguishes it from the other regions of Iraq.

Geographically, the Kurdistan Region of Iraq embodies three governorates: Erbil, Duhok, and Sulaymaniyah, under the control and governorship of the Kurdish Regional Government (KRG). In addition, in the Iraqi Constitution (2005), Article 140 was especially identified to address the disputed land issue between the KRG in Erbil and the federal government in Baghdad; The disputed areas are in the provinces of Diyala, Kirkuk, Nineveh, and Saladin (Washington Kurdish Institute, 2021). The Erbil governorate is the capital of the Kurdish Regional Government. The city had been the principal stop on the Silk Road and is among the oldest inhabited cities in the world. It has also been a famous arena for humanitarian organizations due to its size and stability.

The Kurdish region of Iraq is four times the surface area of Lebanon and more extensive than the Netherlands (Fig. 4), which could make the region the world's eighth-largest oil reserve had it been fully independent and internationally recognized (Ismael, 2020). By the end of 2021, the KRG Ministry of Natural Resources (MNR) estimated the Kurdish region's reserves at 45 billion barrels of oil and 25 trillion cubic feet (Tcf) of proven gas reserves, or around 25% of Iraq's total. It also has up to 198 Tcf of unproven gas (Baram, 2022).

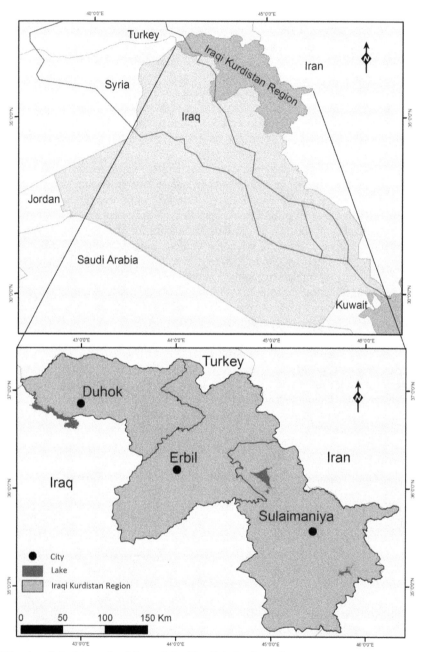

Fig. 4. Administrative Map of the Kurdish Region of Iraq. *Source*: Mohammed et al. (2019).

## 4.2. How Does the KRI's Hydrocarbon Secure International Support?

Inflation and rising fuel prices, especially in Europe, are among the most significant consequences of the Russo–Ukrainian War that began on February 24, 2022 (Cousin, 2023). Achieving energy security at the global level remains a primary priority for all countries to maintain their stability and enhance their security, which creates a real challenge, especially in light of the growing demand for energy (oil and gas) in the first place, which is offset by a decline in supply due to the difference in energy strategies and policies adopted by countries. This has led to an escalation of competition between the major countries, whose policy priorities are the continuous and increasing flow of energy. Thus, today, the primary driver of conflicts has become closely linked to the "geopolitics of energy," and "energy" has become the fuel of many conflicts worldwide.

The natural source (oil and gas) embedded in the region's geographical position has transformed the autonomous territory into a point of attraction for other countries in the Eastern Mediterranean (especially Turkey and Greece), Europe, and even the United States of America. Being under the autonomous KRG has led to relative stability and peace in the region compared to Iraq's parent state. Irrespective of the political instability in Iraq, the KRG has created economic and diplomatic relations with Turkey, Europe, the United States, China, and other countries worldwide. Turkey has a high affinity for the Kurdistan oil and gas primarily as a transition route to Europe and to eliminate their internal scarcity. Nevertheless, Turkey launched a historic 50-year agreement pipeline deal in 2013, ensuring Turkish Energy Company licenses for 12 exploration blocks in the Kurdistan region. The pipeline that carries Kurdish oil to Türkiye's Ceyhan port became operational in 2014, so the KRG has appeared as a significant exporter of oil and gas to Turkey and the European market through the Ceyhan port in the Eastern Mediterranean (Alaaldin, 2023).

Azerbaijan has also emerged as a new supplier to Europe. It is drawing in Kurdistan to partake in the trans-Anatolian natural gas pipeline to reinforce the Shah-Deniz gas field pipeline, which was designed to transport natural gas to Southern European countries. The scarcity of energy supply and the quest to jettison Russia's monopoly in the European market is the biggest worry for Europe.

As a solution to the above predicament, the European Union has embarked on diversifying supplier countries and routes for natural gas, making Kurdistan important for Southeastern Europe and the EU in general. Therefore, from 2007 onwards, substantial international oil and gas companies like Exxon Mobil, Genel Energy, Dana Gas, Total, British Petroleum, BOTAS, and Gazprom have established economic agreements with the KRG for the exportation of oil and gas (Ismael, 2020). The geographical position of a country can be advantageous, as is the case with the KRI.

However, the Kurdistan Region of Iraq is geographically landlocked with no water bodies that can help link it directly to the main markets along or across the Mediterranean via transport by the sea. It is therefore blurring as to the strategy or role played by the KRG in the oil and gas landscape. Here, the critical point is that in Iraq, one religious and ethnic community has always oppressed another. Iraq has also not played a role as a state and institution since 2003. So that the Kurdish officials were viewing their oil and gas sector attract global and regional powers to support their historical Kurdish dream and issue (Paasche & Mansurbeg, 2014).

The Kurdistan region is the border with Iran to the east, currently being sanctioned by the international community; Syria to the west of the region under aggravated civil war from 2011 to present in a deeply divided society; and with the south and southwest by Iraq, controlled by the centralized government in Baghdad which has constantly been in dispute over territory, degrees of autonomy gotten by the KRG, its budget, and power as well as the quest to control the oil and gas reserves in the KRI. With this utterly landlocked territory, the greatest challenge of the KRG is the possibility of exporting oil and gas out of the region to international markets. But with Iranian support, Baghdad is trying to keep the Kurdistan Region away from the energy issue. These factors arguably impede satisfactory agreement for the Kurdish Regional Government over transport routes. As a result of the geopolitical mix-up, the KRG is left with one easy option, Turkey, in the north viable and reliable partner for the export of KRG's natural resources (Alaaldin, 2023).

Again, we cannot set aside the fact that the Kurdistan Region is still officially part and parcel of the Republic of Iraq, which is trapped in a perpetual geopolitical power struggle of sectarian nature in the Middle East region spreading from Iran to Lebanon and Yemen. Therefore, this posed a problem in negotiating new alliances within this tense atmosphere and warranted the KRG to endeavor and demand consideration of rational nature. What sensible considerations can be put in place to minimize the above predicament to guarantee the smooth exportation of oil and gas by the KRG authority? The next paragraphs will focus on the response to the question.

## 4.3. The Reality of the Crude Oil and Gas Production Industry in the Kurdistan Region; Iraq's Unstable

Unreservedly, Article 117 of the Iraqi Constitution (2005) recognizes "Kurdistan" as a federal region having an autonomous government. The "KRG" has official institutions, such as ministries and parliament. The Iraqi Federal Government and KRG share policy-making on water, health, and education and decision-making on the public sectors, which is de-centralized to the KRG (Aresti, 2016).

Systematically, the oil and gas sector of the KRI has marvelously developed after 2003 and has signed about 60 production sharing contracts (PSCs) with international oil companies (IOCs), so many reasons are advanced to justify why these IOCs are being attracted into the Kurdistan oil and gas sector (Heshmati & Auzer, 2019). There is a progressive growth in its oil production, and 430,000 barrels of oil per day will be exported in 2021 (Rudaw, 2021).

Contrary to the instability in Iraq, the maintenance of relative peace and security in the Kurdistan Region has permitted the regional government to embark on oil sector developmental projects and the leasing of land to international and local companies for exploration. According to the PSC, the host state gives a specific area or field to the oil companies, and the government does not assume any financial risk initially. Once the company can extract oil and the wells are commercially helpful, the host state or government determines its shares, property, taxes, and production costs. Conversely, if the oil company cannot discover enough oil to be commercially viable, it will take all the responsibility and leave (Heshmati & Auzer, 2019).

The oil and gas sector of the Kurdish Region of Iraq has grabbed significant political and strategic attention in recent years, because the sector has contributed efficaciously to the economy of the region and also due to the ongoing turmoil in the Iraqi government, the KRG has also taken advantage in oil and gas activities. The region's telecommunications and housing, electricity, healthcare, water supply, and education are being developed thanks to the oil and gas industry. As well as the oil and gas process was also caused by increased internal political conflict, lack of transparency, and social injustice simultaneously.

In a discussion by Auzer (2016), it was highlighted that Iraq's primary hydrocarbon basins are situated in strategic locations: the Zagros fold belt (in the Kurdistan region), the Widyan Basin interior platform (in the western desert), and the Mesopotamia Foredeep (in central and southern Iraq). The Zagros and Taurus fold belts, housing the resources of the Kurdistan region, boast approximately 45 billion barrels of oil reserves. If the region were an independent country, it could rank among the top 10 wealthiest nations in terms of oil and gas reserves (Auzer, 2016).

The production capacity of crude oil operating in the Kurdish Regional Government areas was far more than 500,000 barrels per day in December 2015, evaluated on monthly average basis. However, this production capacity experienced a significant drop on October 16, 2017, due to the invasion and subsequent capture of the Kirkuk's oil fields by the Iraqi military that has been under the control of the KRG since the broke out of the Islamic State in Iraq and Syria in 2014 (Heshmati & Auzer, 2019).

Subsequently, one of the main problems started when Britain and France divided the legacy of the Ottoman Empire in the region after WWI based on oil and natural resources. However, Turkey is still involved in the matter of Kurdistan and Kirkuk's oil, in addition to the fact that ISIS blew up the Kirkuk-Ceyhan oil pipeline in 2014. Since then, the Kirkuk oil has been transported to Turkey's Ceyhan port through the Kurdistan pipeline, and from there, buyers transport it to the global market.

## 4.4. The KRI's Oil and Gas Blocks

There are various ways to categorize the oil and gas fields in the KRI. It may depend on their current situation, such as whether the field is actively producing or still being developed…etc. Moreover, the quantity of production and reserves may serve as a benchmark for their classification. Additionally, the fields could be divided into groups based on how certain they are of their reserves, resources, and activities, as some of the fields are more certain than others about their reserves. As a result, an effort is made to classify the fields using those criteria. Those criteria were taken into account when classifying the fields.

There are 52 oil blocks in Kurdistan Region, and currently, only 9 are in production; 8 of the leading oil block production is in Erbil province. To this effect, the KRI's oil and gas blocks will be classified as follows:

### 4.4.1. Major Fields

The major fields are considered the largest significant oil and gas reserves, and there is some certainty about their future.

#### 4.4.1.1. Tawke and Peshkabir field

Tawke oil field is located in Duhok province. The Tawke field produced about 109,000 barrels of oil daily in July 2017. However, since then, its output has steadily declined, reaching 88,000 in April 2018 and 80,000 in October 2018. At the end of 2011, DNO (Norwegian oil and gas firm) put 13 wills in this field into production, and they continue to effectively contribute about 20% of the KRI's total oil production. Additionally, the field's operator is a transparent corporation (DNO) that frequently discloses and updates information about its reserves and output (Mediterranean Institute for Regional Study, 2019). Peshkabir is located in the western part of the Tawke PSC; the Gross production at the Tawke and Peshkabir license averaged 107,090 bopd in 2022. In the Q2 of 2023, there was no production due to the closed KRI's export pipeline (Genel Energy, 2023).

#### 4.4.1.2. Khurmala Field

Khurmala Dom is the northern section of the Kirkuk field and is located 35 km southwest of Erbil, the capital of the KRI. The field is one of the other main oil fields in the KRI in Erbil Province. It has been under the control of the KRG since 2007. The KAR Group, a Kurdistan-based oil services company, operates the field. Transparency and access to data in this company are complex and almost locked. According to the Wood Mackenzie Report, processing capacity at the field is 200,000 b/d following an expansion in 2018. Oil is delivered to the Erbil refinery and the export terminal at Ceyhan via Kurdistan (Mediterranean Institute for Regional Studies, 2019).

#### 4.4.1.3. Shaikan Field

This is also one of the largest oil discoveries in the Kurdistan Region of Iraq and has been in production since July 2013. As of March 2023, Gulf Keystone Petroleum and MOL Hungarian oil and gas firm are the operators of the Shaikan Field, situated around 60 km to the northwest of Erbil, the largest city in the Kurdistan Region of Iraq, covering an area of 280 km$^2$. In December 2018, the field produced 32,000 bpd, and in the Q1 of 2023, increased the average production to

55,000 bpd, with gross average production increasing by 40% between 2018 and 2022 (Gulf Keystone Petroleum, 2023).

*4.4.1.4. Khor Mor Field*
It's the largest non-associated gas field in Iraq, administratively located in the Sulaymaniyah province, southwest of Chamchemal district and the epicenter of the Qadir Karam sub-district. In 2007, Dana Gas and Crescent Petroleum (UAE energy service firm) signed a contract with the KRG for the exclusive rights to assess, develop, produce, market, and sell hydrocarbons from the Khor Mor and Chemchemal fields in the Kurdistan Region of Iraq (KRI). This agreement gave rise to the Kurdistan Gas Project. Khor Mor supplies Chemchemal and Hawler Electric Power Plants with natural gas. Its daily gas production until August 2018 was about 305 Mscf and 13,000 bpd condensate (Mediterranean Institute for Regional Studies, 2019). In the Q1 of 2023, Dana Gas announced the production average increased to 500 Mscuf, aiming to reach 600 Mcf per day in 2024 (Dana Gas Official Statement, 2023).

As tensions in Iraq escalate, attacks on the Kurdistan Region's oil and gas fields become an expected topic; Khor Mor has suffered from rocket and drone attacks by the Iraqi Shitee Militia due to the close geographic connective of the field, which was struck three times in 2022 and 2023 (Alaaldin, 2023).

*4.4.1.5. Atrush Oil Field*
Atrush oil field is one of the leading new KRI oil fields, located near Duhok province and 85 km northwest Erbil; production started in 2017, operating by The Atrush production sharing license was previously owned by Abu Dhabi National Energy Company – TAQA (39.9%), KRG (25%), ShaMaran Petroleum (20.1%), and Marathon Oil (15%). In July 2017, the field produced around 27,000 bpd (Mediterranean Institute for Regional Studies, 2019). According to the ShaMaran report published on May 10, 2023, in the Q1 of 2023, the gross average production of approximately 66.8 Mbopd {Thousand Barrels of Oil Per Day}, and the level Increased Q1 2023 oil sales to $43.4 million, 12% more than Q1 2022 (ShaMaran Petroleum Report, 2023).

## 4.5. Mid-Sized and Less Productive Fields

Apart from the main influential oil and gas fields, several other oil blocks are under the control of the KRI, which are considered mid-sized, less productive, and promising fields. Most of them are examined following.

Firstly, the Taq Taq license area has a tedious story compared to other KRI fields; the block has a relatively long production history, and it is operated by Genel Energy and started producing in 2006, reaching a record high of roughly 140,000 bpd in 2015. The Taq Taq licensing area is 120 km northwest of the Sulaimaniyah province, 60 km northeast of the Kirkuk oil field, and 85 km southeast of Erbil. The Taq Taq licensed area has a gross size of about 951 square kilometers. According to the company's report, the field has been experiencing geological problems for years. Therefore, the production level has decreased remarkably, averaging 3,610 bopd in Q1 2023! (Genel Energy, 2023).

Chia Surkh is one of the oldest oil wells in the Middle East, located in the village of Chia Surkha in Garmian. The field was discovered and operated in 1901 by the Anglo-Iranian Oil Company. The Chia Surkh oil field is operated by Petoil Turkish company, consistently producing 2,000–3,000 bpd between 2020 and 2022; the company halted its operation in the Chia Surkh on August 1, 2023, due to the decision of the International Court of Arbitration in Paris to stop the KRI's oil export. Petoil is the first oil company to enter the Kurdistan Region of Iraq. In January 2003, Petoil signed a PSA with the KRG, covering a large area, which was subsequently reduced to the current Shakal Block (Petoil, 2023).

The north of Kalar Bawanoor, Sarqala, and Shekh Tawil subdistricts is covered by a Garmian block close to 1780 square kilometers with an estimated oil of about 33 million barrels and 24 bcm or 847 billion cubic feet (bcf) of gas. Gazprom Neft is the operator of the Garmian block with a 40% stake, Western Zagros Ltd with 45%, and the KRG back-in interest (B.I.) 20% thoroughly carried. Repsol (Talisman) has 40% of this block, and Western Zagros B.I. has 40% and 20% wholly carried to the KRG (Salih & Yamulki, 2020).

In addition, several additional KRI fields could receive funding and development to reach the point of production in the ensuing years. Relatively abundant reserves of some of these fields, installed infrastructures, and the upward trend of oil prices may reinforce these fields' future. Among those fields, Kurdamire possesses appropriate contingent petroleum resources of 366 million barrels of oil and 1.8 Tcf of natural gas.

Chemchemal is another promising field with proved and probable condensate reserves of 119 million oil barrels and 6.6 Tcf of natural gas, and Miran with contingent oil resources of 23 million and 6.6 Tcf of natural gas. In addition, Bina Bawi also possesses a contingent oil resource of 37 million oil barrels and 8.2 Tcf of natural gas besides Benenan, with proven and probable oil reserves of 57 million. If these fields are brought to an adequate production level, they may ramp up overall KRI oil production to around 500,000 bpd and 1.5 bcf of gas (Mediterranean Institute for Regional Studies, 2019).

Last but not least is the Erbil block, located in the western part of the KRI, covering the northwest of Erbil and the Bastora area. This block is 313 square kilometers with an estimated 1 billion oil barrels (Salih & Yamulki, 2020). Conflict over hydrocarbon may sometimes emanate depending on the differences in the resource characteristics. The KRI's valued natural resources, which are not renewable, are primarily located in an area geographically limited. Hence, the location with types of resources is vulnerable to conflicts (Lujala & Rustad, 2011).

## 4.6. The KRI's Energy Chessboard: A Call for Realism and Superpower

According to systematic approaches in the international relations literature, particularly the "neorealist theory," which assumes that threats come from abroad and emphasizes the nature of the international system, anarchism, interests, and the struggle for power are the main characteristics of the international political arena (Behravesh, 2010). Hence, Iraq and the Kurdistan Region were facing regional changes, with the "gas and oil" issue serving as the catalyst. As a result, the Kurds must take ownership of their political and economic issues by participating in various ways on the regional chessboard. Petroleum processes include not only "contracting, exploration, extraction, and refining," but also the following phases: export routes (energy geopolitics), lobbying, research on the global economic market, public relations, and its political implications. More importantly, assuming the end of the oil and gas phase, how will their political economy be sustained later?

One of the key assumptions in this chapter of the study is that the Iraqi Kurdistan Region will become a regional player through natural gas and oil and then enter the global energy map. In Iraq, Syria, Turkey, and Iran, Kurds still lack an independent political state. "In Iraqi federalism, there is only one region: the Iraqi Kurdistan Region." The President and Prime Minister of the KRG have been warmly welcomed by heads of countries and high institutions. Also ranging from the Gulf countries to the United Kingdom, United States, and France, they have also delivered numerous speeches and interviews at various levels at international summits (Kurdistan Regional Government, 2023).

In the Middle East, there are two sensitive issues. The first is the issue of combating violence and terrorism, the solution to which is to improve coexistence and combat terrorism. The second matter is considering oil and natural gas. As a result, the Kurdistan Region faced the Islamic State of Iraq and the Syria (ISIS) as a significant force from 2014 to 2017, and terrorism remains a persistent threat to the region as a whole. In addition, on the KRI's territory, religious and minority ethnic communities such as Yazidis, Christians, Turkmen, Arabs, and Shabaks are also protected.

In terms of energy, the Kurdistan Region will export 45,000 barrels of oil per day in 2022 through the Kurdistan–Ceyhan Turkish Pipeline in the Mediterranean Sea and then to global markets (Alhurra, 2023). When the world was suffering from a natural gas crisis in early 2023, the KRI's gas production set a new record. Dana Gas, one of the five companies formed by the Pearl Petroleum Consortium, announced that "production in the Khor Mor gas field had exceeded 500 million cubic feet per day," with plans to reach 1 billion cubic feet of natural gas per day in 2025 (Dana Gas Official Statement, 2023). In addition, three other fields in the KRI produce natural gas; Bina Bawi, Miran, and Khurmala.

The KRG's energy sector, on the other hand, faces significant challenges: As pro-Iranian groups have dominated the Iraqi government, economic, and military sectors since the fall of Saddam Hussein in 2003, the Iraqi central government has opposed the Kurdistan Region's oil processes from the outset; claiming that "Kurdistan oil is being sold to Israel" and that "the Kurdistan Region is a position for Israel and the US to attack Iran from." In reality, Iraq and Iran want to keep the Kurds out of the energy debate (Salih, 2022). As a result, from 2007 to 2023, the KRG oil will be sold in global markets at a lower price than other countries' oil prices in order to attract buyers; which means that oil importers and buyers continue to be hesitant to purchase oil from the KRG (Wahab, 2023).

The Kurdistan Region shares a 513-km border with Iran's Islamic Republic. Furthermore, Iran has a cultural, military, political, and economic hegemony in Iraq. Iran does not want to develop an alternative energy source to supply oil and gas in the region (Salih, 2022). So, when it comes to exporting natural gas from the Kurdistan Region to Europe, the KRI's energy fields are subjected to missile attacks by Iraqi Shiite militia forces, with four separate missile attacks on the Khor Mor gas field in 2022 alone (Wahab, 2023).

As stated by Smeeknens and Keil (2022), in the Federalism Institute at Fribourg University, the Federal Supreme Court in Baghdad ruled on February 15, 2022, that "the KRG's Oil and Gas Law is unconstitutional, citing Articles 110, 111, 112, 115, 121, and 130 of the 2005 Iraqi Constitution" (Smeeknens & Keil, 2022). However, the Federal Supreme Court and its composition are unconstitutional under the constitution referred to by the Federal Court. According to Section 2 of Article 92, the Federal Supreme Court is made up of two-thirds of the members of parliament. As a result, the court is unconstitutional. Article 87 also states the independency and impartiality of the members of the judiciary and the courts in general (Iraqi Constitution of 2005). It is seemingly known that "the decision of the Federal Supreme Court of Iraq was political, and to be used for political purposes and negotiating cards on the tables."

Iraq still needs oil and gas laws. What will the oil and gas law do for Iraq? Is Iraq still in the process of passing the oil and gas law, or is the explosion of the political and social situation in Iraq and foreign intervention decisive this time, and Iraq is in the recovery room and under intensive surveillance?

Iran generally regards Iraq as its hegemonic zone. However, Turkey and the UAE are involved in it, and the US administration backs it up. "The USA funded $250 million to the Khor Mor gas field in 2022 to expand plants and accelerate production" (Rudaw, 2023).

In 2021 and 2022, Iraq (without the Kurdistan region areas) needs 35,000 megawatts of electricity and the electricity demand is constantly increasing, but has yet to be able to produce more than 20,000 megawatts. Iraqi government depends on Iran for a third of its electricity. In addition, "importing gas from Iran to Iraq has a higher price than the global market" (Argus, 2022). However, in January 2023, the Iraqi Oil Ministry announced that proven oil reserves had increased by 6 billion barrels and proven natural gas reserves had increased by 23 billion cubic feet as a result of exploration in the western desert by the Iraqi Oil Ministry's General Oil Exploration Companies, with proven oil reserves had reached 151 billion barrels (Shafaq News, 2023). Accordingly, the biggest gas reserves are in western Iraq's Sunni province of Anbar. This probably increases the interference of Sunni countries in the region.

As Kenneth Waltz, the father of the Neorealism School, pays more attention to powers and the reality of power relations as a prominent factor in international relations; structural realism or "neorealism" is an approach to international relations that confirms the role of "power politics" in international relations, views conflict, and competition as the two main characteristics, and believes that cooperation has limited possibilities. According to Waltz, "competition" and "conflict" are the core of international relations. Also, the distribution of power among countries and the existing anarchic state of international relations literature are considered the two main pillars of international politics. The absence of a higher authority to settle international conflicts is anarchy.

For this reason, neorealism is divided into offensive realism and defensive realism. In these two types, the reality of the regional and international systems is anarchy, and should anarchy come to happen? Because each country is struggling to gain more economic, political, military, and diplomatic power, this is true that causes anarchy. However, ultimately it will be the reason for embodying "security and stability." Therefore, the principle of this international chaos must be decentralized, which means that it should not be gathered power in one center or in one specific point. The reality of offensive realism insists that the state must gain power and create this chaos to impose its dominance through the power and provide security. Nevertheless, defensive realism confirms that this anarchy structure should encourage the state to protect the balance of power and security more softly (Behravesh, 2010, pp. 1–6).

## 4.7. Iron Is Hammered When Hot: The KRI Required to Remain Sold

Spread over the sovereign states of Turkey, Iran, Iraq, and Syria, Kurds are the most significant ethnic minority in the Middle East. The demise of Saddam Hussein made them the primary beneficiaries in Iraq, and the collapse of Syria empowered them to carve out an autonomous region. With their political differences, there is an increasing sentimental attachment between them with moral, material, and human resources shared between Kurds in Turkey, Iraq, Iran, and Syria. Their political ideals are intrinsically linked to each other in all these countries (Yildiz, 2017).

After the WWI, South Kurdistan (Northern Iraq) was annexed to the Iraqi territory to form the Iraqi state. From 1921 to 2022, the Kurdish entity in the region was in war and conflict with successive Iraqi governments. In 1975, Saddam Hussein's regime in Iraq signed the Algiers Agreement with Iran to end the Kurdistan armed revolution. Five years later, Iraq refused to meet Iran's demands, and the Iran–Iraq war (1980–1988) broke out. In 1988, Saddam Hussein's regime killed more than 200,000 Kurds and destroyed their villages (known as the Anfal process). During the Second Gulf War, Saddam Hussein's regime invaded and occupied Kuwait.

As the world entered a new phase, the Cold War ended, the Berlin Wall fell, and the Second Gulf War ended. The global atmosphere became more open under the leadership of the United States, and this led to another Kurdish uprising against the oppressive Ba'athist institutions in 1991, and the United States, Britain, and France for northern Iraq established no-fly zones. On April 5, 1991, the UN Security Council adopted Resolution 688, which states in its preamble: The Council bears full responsibility for ensuring world peace and security and expresses concern about the repression of the Iraqi people.

During the outbreak of the Arab Spring in 2011, the regime of Bashar al-Assad in Syria lost control of its territory. Therefore, the Kurds in Syria were able to create military forces and various political and cultural institutions, with the support of the United States and its allies, to create a kind of autonomy for themselves in Syria. Later, in 2014, when the Islamic State in Iraq and Syria (ISIS) was formed and became a threat to global and regional security, the Kurds in Iraq and Syria became the leading force in the fight against terrorism in the region (Frappi, 2016).

Thus, the issue of energy and the fight against terrorism has advanced the Kurdish issue in the international community. Of course, Iran has significant interests with a strong presence in Iraq and will not allow the Kurdistan Region's natural gas to replace the Iranian gas in the region. As an influential regional power, Turkey needs oil and natural gas to meet its domestic needs. Without its signature, it will not allow the Kurdistan Region or West Kurdistan (Northern Syria) to reach the Mediterranean basin for energy.

In short, the birth and growth of the KRGs stemmed from the regional change consequences; the KRG's weakening and disappearance would also be due to global change. Likewise, the shape can be changed when a hot iron is beaten with a hummer; after the fall of Saddam Hussein in 2003, the Kurds were strong in Iraq, and the central government did not have an oil and gas law. However, when the Kurdish position in Iraq weakened in 2023, Baghdad took steps to intensify its efforts to pass an Iraqi oil and gas law.

## 4.8. Can Natural Gas Become a Turning Point in the Geopolitics of the KRG?

The leadership of the KRG has made use of this regional autonomy by having opted for choices that have set its oil industry on a very different path from that of the Baghdad's central government. Although the KRG was constitutionally recognized in 2005, Baghdad insisted that all production and oil exploitation contracts must be structured in partnership with the central government. The KRG refuted this position and proceeded to sign more than fifty contracts with IOCs from 2006 to 2013, all considered illegal by Baghdad. This economic behavior of aggressive nature from Baghdad aroused the KRI population to believe that the time of an independent Kurdistan was drawing near, which was also being encouraged by medical houses worldwide. Due to this antagonism between the KRG and Baghdad over absolute control of the hydrocarbon, the KRI saw this as an opportunity, quickly reinforcing its historical trajectory and gathering more aspirations for self-determination (Klich, 2013).

This relation has appeared to fuel and foster the Iraqi Kurds' economic autonomy. Turkish businesses are being invested in the autonomous Kurdish Region of Iraq, which has developed into a thriving trade relationship, with US$12 billion in the KRG-Turkey trade in 2011. To this effect, the Turkish trade with Syria, Lebanon, and Jordan was lesser than the trade with the KRG in 2010, becoming a center of the KRG's economic future and a more significant opportunity for potential independence (Dargin, 2007).

The KRG has and is in control of its security force and military, maintains border crossings, and among other things, the KRI has the power to enact legislation on issues where the federal laws of Iraq are silent, and the KRI's hydrocarbon resources act as a motivation contributing efficaciously to the visible potential independence of the KRI in numerous parameters (Mills, 2016).

Firstly, the existence of the KRI autonomous power – born from a conflict that was arguably triggered by the abundant hydrocarbon resources in the KRI – has now given the KRG the right to enter into, sign, and approve oil and gas contracts with influential international companies. This encouraged many oil and gas companies to shift from Baghdad to the KRG. A glaring example is when American independent oil firm Hess was prohibited from getting the most recent licensing from Iraq when it signed a PSC with the KRG.

The KRG has used its autonomous power to put in place favorable exploration terms for firms, pushing some firms, including ExxonMobil and Total, to shift allegiances toward the KRG (Gray, 2012). The KRG has gained some support in developing their oil and gas reserves from Europe and the United States in trying to counterweight Russian gas. In the words of the director of gas research at the Oxford Institute for Energy Studies, Jonathan Stern, "Russian reserves overwhelm all other gas reserves available to Europe except reserves from the Middle East countries."

Russia is the source from which the vast majority of European natural gas is being piped. In trying to jettison this effect, the European Union and the United States are planning to establish a pipeline that, if realized, will transport Kurdish gas directly to European markets. This project will increase interdependency between Iraqi Kurdistan and the European Union while waiving any control from Baghdad. The Kurdish will then gain an outlet for their natural gas that will no longer be transported through the Kirkuk–Ceyhan pipeline (often controlled by Iraq) to Turkey. This will limit Baghdad's ability to undercount its exports and withhold its gas revenues, which may give the KRG more aspirations for potential independence (Mills, 2016).

On the other hand, within the context of the Iraq–Kurdish conflict, controlling the hydrocarbon-rich area means controlling the political and economic power. Therefore, the control over oil flow was never limited to financial gain, because it is also an indication of influence over political power and the control of the land. The oil flow under the control of KRG has led to the essential economic motivation behind the KRI's diplomatic and military efforts. This gives a reasonable explanation for the fact that, after the demise of Saddam Hussein's government, Kirkuk's oil was a bone of contention among the Iraqi government. The KRG, had it been the oil under the control of the KRI, would have gained an essential economic and political instrument in its quest for Kurdish autonomy and subsequent independence.

Caspersen has propagated five characteristics for a territory to be considered a de facto state: The territory must be in control of the majority of its claimed territory; external and internal legitimacy must be increased by building state institutions; a clear demonstration of the aspiration for independence or a formal declaration of independence; the territory is still void of international recognition, and the territory must have existed for at least two years (Palani et al., 2021).

In general, the issue of Kurdistan's natural gas, both as an opportunity for further support to the Kurdistan Region and as a geopolitical turning point, includes the following points:

First, gas is a more critical turning point than oil. Despite several political events from 2011 to 2022, the energy issue in the Kurdistan Region has proven to be multidimensional and very complex. For the Kurds, the oil and gas issue has always been viewed not only as an energy or financial source but also from many other perspectives.

Second, the question is whether the dramatic changes will change the historical situation of the Kurds. This requires an understanding of two essential stages. The first is the Kurdistan Region's reliance on its agreement with Turkey, signed in early November 2013 and known locally as the 50-year agreement. The second stage is the war against ISIS. While the target of the war against ISIS was to weaken or even destroy the Kurds, finally, it strengthened the Kurds.

On the other hand, the Kurdistan independence referendum in 2017, which was supposed to strengthen the Kurds, had yet to have the outcome they wanted finally. These two political events have a direct impact on the situation of the KRG and the possibility of change. As a result, the changes in the KRG are an overall process and do not just involve the existence or construction of the energy sector.

Third, we can proclaim, "Welcome to the gas era!" The Russian–Ukrainian war in 2022 has brought more energy geopolitics to the forefront and complicated the condition. The European Union no longer sees Russia as a reliable partner in natural gas after the Ukraine war, so the KRG's Prime Minister Masrour Barzani said that the Kurdistan Region "can help Europe in terms of energy" (Aziz, 2022).

Fourth, regional powers see the development of the Kurdistan gas sector as part of strengthening the KRG. The United States supports the Kurdistan Region's energy sector. For example, the Kor Mor field, one of the KRI's major gas fields, was signed in 2007 between Dana Gas and Crescent Petroleum. The field has 4.3 trillion cubic feet of approved gas. It will produce about 2,000 megawatts of electricity for the Kurdistan Region through three power plants. The United States had allocated $250 million to expand the Kor Mor field earlier. In addition, when the Iraqi Federal Court, on February 15, 2022, ruled that the oil contracts and oil processes in the Kurdistan Region were unconstitutional, it also blacklisted some of the oil companies operating in the Kurdistan Region. The Kurdistan Region called the decision political. The US administration has repeatedly called for a solution to this problem through official and diplomatic means. The lack of institutions in the Kurdistan Region and continued internal divisions have complicated the status. However, the United States has reaffirmed its defense of the Kurdistan Region (Mediterranean Institute for Regional Studies, 2022).

Fifth, the Kurdistan Region is under military, security, and geopolitical pressure from Iran and Iraqi Shitee militia. Iran does not want Kurdistan's natural gas to be treated as a substitute for Iranian energy since that would strengthen Israel.

Russia also opposes exporting energy from the Kurdistan Region to avoid the Mediterranean block. However, as the Deputy Prime Minister of the KRG Qubad Talabani, during the Delphi Economic Forum in Greece on April 6–9, 2022, said, "I asserted that the Kurdistan Region is in front of a historic opportunity to export gas. However, we must resolve our legal issues before anything else." He also pointed out, "We do not doubt that Kurdish gas can contribute and alleviate many problems that the world is facing with gas shortages" (Rudaw, 2022).

Ultimately, the Kurdistan Region of Iraq has owned an oil pipeline built at the end of 2013; Rosneft holds a 60% stake in the pipeline, while KAR Group, an Iraqi Kurdistan-based company, holds the remaining 40%. The concession period is 20 years with an option to extend for 5 years. The pipeline has a designed oil transport capacity of about 950,000 bpd and a length of about 420 km. There needs to be more! These conditions must be established and reorganized for the new KRG's energy vision.

## 4.9. KRG's Oil Flow to the Mediterranean: A Focus on the Future

In a broader geopolitical and global market context, since 2010, natural gas discoveries and extraction in offshore Cyprus, Israel, Lebanon, and Syria have brought prominent geopolitical reverberation. Hence, energy giant corporations flocked to the Eastern Mediterranean as natural gas was discovered. For 11 years, Noble Energy and Exxon Mobile, British Petroleum (BP), French Total, Italian Eni, Israeli Delek Drilling, and the German DEA have devoted their technical, economic, and diplomatic power to pursuing their interests in the Eastern Mediterranean (Mediterranean Institute for Regional Studies, 2022, December 29). Building 1,900 km of underwater pipelines at a cost of about $7 billion to deliver 10 billion cubic meters of natural gas annually from Cyprus and Israel to Europe via Greece has many supporters at the governmental level, both in Greece and abroad (Chondrogiannos, 2022). This gives the impression that a geopolitical and political-economic event is taking place.

Therefore, since 2010, the East-Med gas project has been viewed as an alternative to Russian natural gas in Europe or at least reduces Europe's dependence on Russian energy. Also, the event has turned Israel from an importer of natural gas to an energy exporter! Furthermore, these changes encouraged other regional powers and countries to move the region. For instance, the UAE, although not geographically linked to the Eastern Mediterranean, has joined as a member of the (EMGF) and Israel has sold a 22% stake in the Tamar gas field to the UAE's Mubadala Petroleum for 1.2$billion (Anadolu Agency, 2021). While Turkey is an influential regional power in the eastern Mediterranean and the Middle East, on the one hand, it requires a lot of oil and natural gas to meet its domestic needs. On the other hand, it desires to pass energy pipelines in the region through its territory. Nevertheless, from 2010 to 2022, Turkey has not joined the eastern Mediterranean gas project due to Turkey's stubborn policies toward Greece, Cyprus, Israel, Egypt, and Syria in the last decade.

Iraq, and the Kurdistan region, is the epicenter of a new Silk Road to the Mediterranean. However, it is cumbersome to derogate from the fact that, even though Turkey has complex energy relations with Iraq, it has always been at the forefront of playing a crucial role in the oil and gas development in KRI. Traditionally, the critical aspect of Turkey as a territory in transit of oil from federal Iraq to the Mediterranean is also very significant. It goes with the recent affirmation that while Turkish investors play an enormous role in developing hydrocarbon resources in the KRI, federal Iraq is witnessing Turkish companies constantly seeking significant commercial opportunities in Bagdad (Roberts, 2018). Encouraged by the fact that Northern Iraq is a land-locked territory, its oil transportation has always been successful through transnational pipelines to the coast of the Mediterranean, where it was accessible to the European market.

The production and transportation of Iraq's oil through pipelines via Syria to Europe were controlled by a consortium of British, French, American, and Dutch oil companies under what was known as the Iraq Petroleum Company (IPC) from 1929 to 1972. The Iraq Petroleum Company (IPC) pipelines closed in 1976. This allowed Turkey to develop and stretch its economic tentacles to Iraq in general and the KRI in particular (Bowlus, 2015).

Hydrocarbon resource transactions through the two pipeline projects are not limited to oil and gas. However, a political and economic influence embedded in the energy deal with the KRG is also highly considered. Turkey had to ensure an adequate and permanent energy supply to meet an increase in demand coupled with a fast expansion of its economy. In addition to the fact that Russia and Iran were the only source of Turkey's power generation, the Syrian crisis also acted as a rift between Turkey, Russia, and Iran. This relation allowed the Turkish economy to be trapped by the region's dynamics and price shocks. To remedy these predicaments and decrease its dependency on Iran and Russia, Turkey needed to scramble in search of alternative energy resources. Turkey had no choice but to urgently resolve its Kurdish problem and capitalize on the openings in KRI to cultivate energy ties with the KRG (Tol, 2014).

The Kirkuk-Ceyhan Pipeline, also known as the Iraq-Turkey Pipeline (ITP), the biggest pipeline for transporting crude oil, was targeted by the Islamic State and rendered non-operational (Fig. 5). The Kirkuk-Ceyhan Pipeline allows Kirkuk to export oil over 600 miles from two major hydrocarbon fields in Kirkuk to the Mediterranean port of Ceyhan in southern Turkey (Kraemer, 2019). Recently, negotiations were going on for constructing a new pipeline between Kirkuk and Turkey that will link Kirkuk to the Mediterranean bloc.

This heavy project operated successfully until 1990, when there was an outbreak of war, sanctions, and sabotage by Sunni groups that rendered the pipeline inoperable. Again, the self-styled Islamic State or ISIS interrupted the pipeline and rendered the transportation of crude oil impossible. To minimize this effect, Turkey bypassed Iraq and established a new economic relationship with the KRG in 2013. A new economic partnership was therefore sealed between the KRG and Turkey. This led to the construction of a new pipeline from Khurmala at the head of the Kirkuk oilfield to the Turkish border, which links up with the Turkish section of the original Kirkuk-Ceyhan system (Bowlus, 2015).

Oil and Gas in the Iraqi Kurdistan 81

Fig. 5. The Kirkuk-Ceyhan Oil Pipeline, stretching from northern Iraq to the Turkish Mediterranean coast, spans a length of 600 miles (970 km). Turkey and Iraq reached an agreement in 1973 to construct this pipeline, connecting the Kirkuk fields to the Mediterranean port of Ceyhan in southern Turkey. the pipeline was completed and commissioned in 1977. *Source:* Kirkuk–Ceyhan_oil_pipeline-HE.svg: *Mosul-Haifa_oil_pipeline.svg: Amirki (talk) derivative work: Amirki derivative work: Amirki (https://commons.wikimedia.org/wiki/File:Kirkuk-Ceyhan_oil_pipeline.svg), "Kirkuk–Ceyhan oil pipeline," https://creativecommons.org/licenses/by-sa/3.0/legalcode.

The Khurmala-Ceyhan Pipeline, with an initial capacity of handling 450,000 bpd, was later increased to 700,000 bpd in 2015. The KRG consolidated control over all of the major oilfields in the north, including Bai Hassan and Avana dome, even with the invasion of IS in 2014. This pipeline has permitted the KRI oil and gas transportation from KRI directly to Turkey without any influence from Baghdad, thereby setting up the KRG as a competitive supplier of crude oil to Turkey. This action angered Baghdad, and it immediately responded by filing a request for arbitration against Ankara to the International Commercial Arbitration (ICC) in Paris because Ankara had given Kurds an independent pipeline. According to Baghdad, Ankara has violated the Iraq–Turkish pipeline agreement that was agreed upon in 1973 and updated in 1976, 1985, and 2010 (Knights, 2010).

The KRG has continuously reported exports of 400,000 barrels daily, with an increased capacity of up to 1 million barrels in 2018. This has expanded infrastructure development in the KRI with outflows that could rise to 1.5 million. Baghdad has not only desired to have control of that revenue but has also demanded the distribution of the proceeds based on an agreement with Erbil that has eluded the two governments since the toppling of Saddam Hussein in 2003. Baghdad fears that the KRI can grasp a kind of energy autonomy that would lead to outright political independence if the outcome of the arbitral award is rendered in favor of Turkey (Kraemer, 2019).

The new 2013 oil pipeline, masterminded by Turkey, which runs from Khurmala at the head of the Kirkuk oilfield to the Turkish border, was born from the fact that KRG was prompted to formulate its hydrocarbon law in 2007 after a successive failure of Baghdad and Erbil to reach an agreement on a unified hydrocarbon law. The coming into force of 2007 KRG's on hydrocarbon completely changed the strategy of the major IOCs, altered Kurdish aspirations for autonomy, and changed the landscape for transporting oil from northern Iraq. To this effect, Exxon-Mobil (US), Total (France), Gazprom Neft (Russia), Chevron (US), and TAQA (Abu Dhabi) signed production-sharing contracts for exploratory blocks in the KRI from 2011 to 2012, transporting oil directly from the KRI without any imprimatur from Baghdad (Bowlus, 2015). This has been such that, while Baghdad is still contesting revenue and the demand for distribution of proceeds emanating from the KRI oil, Turkey-KRG crude oil relationship continues to be successful as Turkey is a strategic energy-transit country.

Three reasons are accountable for this successful relationship. First, Turkey's security can perpetually guard a pipeline such that even if opposing groups like the Kurdistan Workers' Party (PKK) were to damage the pipeline, repairs could be made expediently, and pipelines could restart in a matter of days. Secondly, in addition to the fact that Turkey has the largest military in the Middle East, it is willing to employ force when its interests are threatened. Again, the growing economy of Turkey has no meaningful oil of its own, which makes the country eager to secure its demand for oil and gas. Lastly, Turkey can avoid the vicissitudes of intra-Arab politics that have plagued previous transnational pipelines in the region, given that Turkey is a non-Arab country. Therefore, the problem may be interpreted as an internal conflict between Baghdad and Erbil. However, Ankara is an essential factor that can either stabilize or spoil this affair (Natali, 2014).

*Kurdistan can be welcomed by the United States, Europe, and other regional energy blocs like Gulf countries and the Eastern Mediterranean Gas Forum (EMGF).*

In short, because of the regional powers' threats to the KRI's oil and gas fields, the KRI's energy sector requires the support of superpowers such as the United States and Europe. At the same time, political, economic, and social stability in the Kurdistan Region cannot be achieved without internal reforms. Therefore, the two ruling political parties in the Kurdistan Region must bring a new atmosphere and blur the political disputes to formulate a new energy vision to maintain the KRI's national security.

One of the masterminded scenarios is that energy can always be seen as a common ground. The East Mediterranean gas project will become a more significant global energy bloc and replace Russia's energy to the West. For this purpose, the natural gas and oil of the Kurdistan Region of Iraq and northern Syria are heading to the east of the Mediterranean Sea (this only passes with the security risks of Iran and Russia). Moreover, another Gulf energy line may also reach the Mediterranean Sea on Syrian or Jordanian land.

As Baram (2022) argued, the Kurdistan Region and Iraq are competing with Iran regarding oil exports to Turkey due to the Kurdistan–Ceyhan pipeline. As well as the Kurdish gas alternative will also be more stable and likely cheaper; "the same is true when it comes to Kurdish gas to Turkey." In 2021 and 2022, Iran alone supplied 16% of Turkey's natural gas demands. Kurdish gas supply to Turkey, too, is therefore viewed by Tehran as worrisome competition (Baram, 2022).

Chapter Five

# Intertwining of the New Global and Regional Order in the Mediterranean Region

## Abstract

The Eastern Mediterranean's energy reserves have ushered in a new era of economic, military, and political dynamics, both locally and globally. While the trade in natural gas has reshaped the region's economic landscape, it has also sparked heightened tensions and security concerns. Positioned at the crossroads of Europe, Asia Minor, and Africa, the Eastern Mediterranean now serves as a nexus for political, military, and economic interests. This chapter explores how the region's eastern and southern shores have historically been a battleground for competing political ideologies, economic systems, and military arsenals, notably those of the United States and the Soviet Union. It delves into the complexities of foreign intervention by nations and organizations, with a particular focus on the roles of the United States, Russia, and NATO's Mediterranean Initiative. Additionally, the chapter evaluates the theoretical frameworks of international relations, including neorealism, neoliberal institutionalism, and regional security complex theories, to elucidate the dynamics of hydrocarbon competitions in the Eastern Mediterranean and their implications for energy security.

*Keywords*: Eastern Mediterranean; security system; US Agenda; Russia's presence; theoretical arguments

## 5.1. Highlighting the US Agenda in the Eastern Mediterranean

Since early 2010, the US's giant companies, such as Noble Energy, Chevron, and ExxonMobile, have made a prominent contribution to the Eastern Mediterranean hydrocarbon process. Noble Energy alone managed to obtain a 39.66% stake in the Leviathan gas field, 36% in the Tamar field (Offshore Technology), and a 30% stake in the Cypriot field of Aphrodite (Al-Ghannam, 2022, p. 585). Also, the United States established an American center specializing in the Eastern Mediterranean affairs in June 2019. Its mission is to submit a report to the congress on the action plan of American companies that invest in the energy exploration and development in the Eastern Mediterranean and the facilities granted by the American government to them, as well as the activities of companies affiliated with competing countries.

The goal of the United States – to protect the investments of its companies in the Eastern Mediterranean – was a motive for many American policies in the region, including, for example, the American position on the Lebanese–Israeli conflict over the maritime borders, in which the United States played a mediating role for years without reaching a final solution. Regarding the American position on the conflict, as mentioned above, the proposals submitted by the United States to solve the problem seemed somewhat biased toward the Lebanese side. One of the interpretations of this position was that it reflects the American desire to achieve stability in the region and not to provoke a reaction from the Lebanese Hezbollah, which would threaten the huge US investments in the region (Al-Ghannam, 2022, p. 586).

According to Inbar (2022), for the United States, especially the Biden administration, limiting the attraction of Chinese hegemony and Russia's threat to Europe are top priorities. Meanwhile, rising energy prices, as well as the establishment of political dialogue, joint military exercises, and diplomatic relations in the Mediterranean Sea because of energy between Cyprus, Israel, and Greece makes the United States to consider the importance of this region. In addition, the three states conduct various military exercises and refine their capabilities. Greater interaction in other areas has cemented this equality, which has political and strategic consequences. For instance, it changed Turkey's policy toward Israel parallel to the Abraham Accords (Inbar, 2022).

Solving the Syrian crisis and managing the US growing policy divergence with Turkey is at the center of the US foreign policy in the Mediterranean (Alterman et al., 2018). However, another US strategic interest is promoting alliance between the Eastern Mediterranean states. It is unlikely for the United States as a world power to be uninterested in the energy potentials in the Eastern Mediterranean (Demir & Tekir, 2017). Generally, the United States has demonstrated less strategic interest toward the Eastern Mediterranean region in the last decade. Though the US foreign policies engulf the Eastern Mediterranean, the US diplomacy and interest in this region has been that of a ping pong. Meanwhile, the United States indicated some interest in the Eastern Mediterranean as far back as 1947 under the Truman administration when the threat of intervention by the Soviet Union was imminent.

During the different US administrations, the Eastern Mediterranean region has had various geopolitical, economic, and security importance; since the US withdrawal from the region and the weakening of Russia will give Turkey and other regional powers more freedom to operate. Demir and Tekir (2017) have suggested that the rationale for the US nonchalant interest in the region is the fact that US recent development of its natural gas sector and new attention to Iran. Even though the United States is said to be reluctant about the Eastern Mediterranean region, the presence and contribution of the US-based company, Noble Energy in the discovery, exploration, and production of natural gas in the region has been a massive one. Here, we face a problem and a question that we need to deal with about the US presence in the region. Is this existence based on providing regional peace and security and upholding environmental issues, or is it just related to giant companies and the biggest banks?

Here, a different understanding of history needs to advocate the emergence of a new regional paradigm, as it sparked through the EMGF. This was a step toward a regional cooperation system that included Egypt, Israel, Jordan, Cyprus, Greece, Italy, France, the Palestinian Authority, and even the UAE. However, on January 9, 2022, the United States sent a semi-official letter to the foreign ministries of Israel, Cyprus, and Greece; informing them that the United States would withdraw its support from the gas pipeline project in the Eastern Mediterranean. Earlier, the United States had suddenly withdrawn from Afghanistan and claimed to leave the Middle East. A month later, the war in Ukraine broke out, increasing the energy prices, and the influence of Russia, China, and Iran became more apparent. Then we saw that the United States had suffered from strategic miscalculations and short-sightedness.

### 5.1.1. The United States and Prospects for a New Regional Security System in the Eastern Mediterranean

Since 2011, the US naval exercises have been operational in the Eastern Mediterranean maritime zones with the active involvement of both the Greece and Israeli forces. "Noble Dina" has been the main of such exercises and the US navy has defined it as a joint exercise aimed at fostering interoperability by building individual and collective maritime expertise of participating countries, as well as encouraging amity, shared understanding, and collaboration (Cropsey, 2015).

Initially, the first trilateral summit between Greece, Israel, and Cyprus was held in January 2016. Then the leaders' decision emerged to create a committee to plan a pipeline to transport natural gas from Israel to Europe. In June 2017, Italy became part of this process and a working group was established to oversee the project. On January 2, 2020, the East-Med Pipeline as a strategic agreement was signed in Athens by the leaders of Israel, Greece, and Cyprus (NS Energy, 2021).

In 2019, representatives of the four states, that is the United States, Israel, Greece, and Cyprus reunited in Jerusalem to affirm their shared commitment to promoting peace, stability, security, and prosperity in the Eastern Mediterranean. During their meeting, the US Secretary of State, Mike Pompeo, reaffirmed the US support for the trilateral mechanism established by Israel, Greece, and Cyprus; upholding it to be a vital tool for further cooperation (The US Embassy in Athens, 2019). The leaders agreed to increase regional cooperation, to support energy independence and security, and to defend against external malign influences in the Eastern Mediterranean and the broader Middle East. They welcomed the recent natural gas finds in the Eastern Mediterranean and its potential to contribute to energy security and diversification.

As a further sign of consolidation of the United States backing to Cyprus, Greece, and Israeli Trilateral relationship, the US Congress met and passed a bill in 2019; known as the Eastern Mediterranean Security and Energy Partnership Act, aimed at promoting security and energy partnerships in the Eastern Mediterranean, and for other purposes repetitious and shallow as stated. In the bill, the key stakeholders to the bill which are the United States, Greece, Cyprus, and Israel affirmed their commitment to

> oppose any action in the eastern Mediterranean and the Aegean Sea that could challenge stability, violate international law or undermine good neighborly relations and in a joint declaration on March 21$^{st}$, 2019, agreed to defend against external malign influences in the Eastern Mediterranean and the broader Middle East. (US Congress, 2019)

According to scholars like Zoppo, the role of the United States in the Eastern Mediterranean region should not be overemphasized as it acts as a conflict manager. He presents that the United States performs as a principal security stakeholder in the Mediterranean. According to Zoppo, the United States is the sole country with the military might to counterbalance the prospective of Russian military hegemony into the region. He further asserts that the United States is the "only Western country that, for the foreseeable future, has the political capacity – through its network of bilateral relations, within and outside NATO, with Mediterranean countries – to bring coherence to the defense of the area" (1982, p. 70).

These mentioned above all together describe the pattern of events: However, in early 2021, Israel and Cypriot gas export began; and in early 2022, the United States suspended its support for the East-Med Gas Pipeline Project. Did the United States embody the region's peace, stability, and prosperity? Is it possible to reduce the Eastern Mediterranean region to just a few companies and the support of Biden's administration?

In fact, the Ukraine crisis reminded us that war is still a policy option, even in Europe. The Eastern Mediterranean and the Middle East are more conflict-ridden and aggressive regions than Europe. Security concerns, immigration, human rights, inequality, climate change and environmental pollution, water delineation, Turkey's incursion into Syria, Israel–Palestine conflict, these and many other problems are waiting to be solved in the region.

*5.1.1.1. The US Policy and Reducing the European Dependency on the Russian Gas*
The United States does not view its interest in gas in the Eastern Mediterranean for American domestic consumption purposes. On the contrary, the data indicate

that the United States may become the biggest gas exporter in the world in the future. Given the discovery of shale gas in the United States, the American interests in the Mediterranean region, in general, are mostly indirect; as the US interest in the region was linked from the beginning to the importance of the region to its allies. Thus, natural gas resources in the Eastern Mediterranean play an essential role in the US policy, as it is an available option to reduce European countries' dependence on Russian gas exports. In this regard, the United States encourages proposed projects to export gas from its sources in the fields of the Eastern Mediterranean to the European Union.

As pointed out by Al-Ghannam (2022), about linked American policy in Iraq and Syria and the US efforts to find sources of gas that reach Europe away from Russia; they interpreted the US insistence on controlling certain areas in Syria and Iraq as a matter that reflects the American goal of extending pipelines to transport oil and gas from Qatar, Saudi Arabia, and Israel through the areas that include US forces in Iraq and northeastern Syria, and may be connected to the Egyptian-Israeli gas line – to and from Turkey(Al-Ghannam, 2022, p. 587).

Despite all of that, the United States is working to link the interests of its allies in the Eastern Mediterranean to each other, so that it creates a regional grouping consisting of gas-producing countries and countries suitable for gas exports to European countries that are also allies of the United States, so that the economies of those countries are linked in a network that guarantees the protection of the American interest in the region. That goal was expressed by the then Vice President Joe Biden in 2015, when he spoke about the American vision in the Eastern Mediterranean, and mentioned the formation of an alliance between Egypt, Israel, Cyprus, Greece, and Turkey to export gas to Europe through pipelines passing through Greece and Turkey (Yegin, 2022). In general, the United States, to achieve its goals in the region, has implemented the following policies:

The United States encouraged the export of Israeli gas to Jordan within the framework of uniting the interests of its allies. In September 2014, Jordan signed an agreement with Israel to purchase gas from the Leviathan field for 15 years at a value of $18 billion. According to this agreement, Jordan became dependent on Israel for 40% of its energy imports (Al-Ghannam, 2022, p. 587).

The United States has also performed to directly supervise the normalization of ties between Israel and Turkey after it reached the point of Turkey expelling the Israeli ambassador and reducing diplomatic representation to the degree of second secretary in 2011 following the "Mavi Marmara ship incident" (Yegin, 2022).

The United States aims to find a solution to the deep-rooted Cyprus problem, and to achieve consensus in relations with Turkish Cypriots, allowing the implementation of several pending power transmission projects that require approval from the TRNC and the Republic of Cyprus. Moreover, Turkey and Cyprus are essential allies of the United States; and the stability of their relationship is directly linked to American interests; both have a strategic position for implementing the US strategic agenda to prevent and encircle Russia's hegemony in the region. For that purpose, the United States begun with the deployment of a series of military bases and spy points which is started from 26 bases in Turkey, and passing through five US military bases in the Iraqi Kurdistan region (according to the Erbil-Washington Protocol in 2016), four bases and airstrips in Iraq (Baghdad, Tallil Air Base, H1, south of Iraq) and the US military bases in Israel; all the way to the British Akrotiri base in the Republic of Cyprus, completing an arc of US military bases to encircle Russia's role in the region (Al-Ghannam, 2022, p. 588).

The United States insisted to confirm its strategic interest in the Eastern Mediterranean Gas Forum (EMGF) through Rick Perry, US Secretary of Energy, who attended the forum meetings in Cairo in July 2019 (Yegin, 2022).

## 5.2. Russian Foreign Policy in the Mediterranean: An Adventure or a New Paradigm?

Particularly since 2011, political tension and conflicts in the Eastern Mediterranean region have made it a center stage for power struggles between many external actors. Just like its counterparts United States and some European countries, Russia has sought to have its own fair share of the Eastern Mediterranean cake. Russia has been skilled and successful in attempting opportunities to engage in the region, cultivating rising political, religious, economic, or cultural decision-makers in Greece, Cyprus, and Turkey. However, there are some differences in policy points between Russia and Turkey: In Libya, Syria, the Caucasus, and Ukraine, but in general, Russia has been able to complicate the equations with Europe and the United States in the region and create a rift in the Western alliances. Ankara's purchase of Russian S-400 missiles is the best evidence, which has largely created a gap between Turkey and NATO as well as Ankara and Washington. This would exclude western Turkey from the Patriot and F-35 missile programs (Sergeyevna, 2020).

According to Clark et al. (2020), Russia's quest to gain more access and a leeway in the Mediterranean region has been consolidated through maintaining and reinforcing a strong military presence in the region. This increasing impact of Russia in the region has strained the US/NATO position in the Eastern Mediterranean region, as trust has shifted from the West wing in favor of Russia. Many authors have suggested that Russia's strong presence in the Eastern Mediterranean is due to the fact that Russia came in to fill the vacuum which had been created in certain Eastern Mediterranean countries. For example, the United States withdrawal from Syria created a great vacuum which Russia took advantage of to win the central stage (Clark et al., 2020).

Since 2015, Russia has launched military operations in Syria, and this contributed to alternating completely Russia's position in the Eastern Mediterranean region. In a guise to reinstate peace and stability in Syria, Russia gave itself a legitimate reason to intervene into Syria. Despite so, Russia's mission became frustrated and unaccomplished. Meanwhile, under the Putin administration, Russia has reemerged and reconsolidated its position in the global stage of politics. For that, the recent trends in the Russian's foreign policy center around the Mediterranean region, especially in the dawn of the monumental hydrocarbon discoveries in the region (Ahmed, 2020).

The military presence is another strategic approach by which Russia gains its position in the Eastern Mediterranean region. Russia for example has maintained a formidable military presence in the northern part of the Eastern Mediterranean through the positioning of a standing army in Syria and the establishment of a nuclear power facility in Turkey. Taking Cyprus as another example, Russia has incessantly expressed interest in the Republic of Cyprus, and consequently, through a military approach, overwhelming attempts have been made by Russia to stiffen the Republic of Cyprus' cooperation with the United States and NATO. Efforts have equally been made by Moscow to establish a strategic but cordial economic relationship with Lebanon and Israel (Ahmed, 2020).

Energy is a vital facet of Russia's strategic foreign policy in the Eastern Mediterranean. In 2013, Russia's Foreign Ministry indicated Russia's energy agenda to fortify its strategic cooperation with key energy producers, while at the same time actively encouraging dialogue with consumers and transit countries. One of Russia's main goals has been to create a liaison with important players in the energy market. That notwithstanding, a wider part of Russia's policy is to enhance price regulation in the oil market to establish a stable price for oil, to involve in the export of nuclear energy as well as to be a part of the projects of exploration, production and exportation of energy (Mamedov, 2021).

In short, during the Ukraine War, the world experienced that it was Russian natural gas that was heating Europe. The West has relied on oil and natural gas from the Middle East and Russia for an extended period. Energy has endangered western symbols and economic infrastructure, and perhaps even the western civilization!

### 5.2.1. Has Russia Succeeded with Its Presence in the Eastern Mediterranean?

Russian interests in the field of energy in the Eastern Mediterranean are represented in two strategic targets: The first is an investment in Russian energy corporations, and the second is to maintain a Russian naval presence in the Mediterranean basin:

*5.2.1.1. The Role of Russian Energy Companies in the Eastern Mediterranean*
According to Rettig et al. (2020), the gas reserves discovered in the Eastern Mediterranean do not threaten Russian hegemony in the European gas markets. Russia exports approximately 200 billion cubic meters of natural gas every year to Europe (even during the start of the Russo–Ukrainian War in 2022); while Israel, for example, has allocated approximately 350–450 billion cubic meters for export over the next 30 years, a quantity that Russia will export within two years, although from that, Russia aims to handle any threat – albeit limited – to its control over the markets of its European power; and this is related to the fact that Russia is a superpower in the field of energy and is fully aware that the pivotal economic pillar is energy exports, and then the rise of any competing power in this field – even if it is small, it undermines this Russian advantage (Rettig et al., 2020).

The mechanism that Russia decided to face any potential competition from gas producers in the Eastern Mediterranean was to pursue two policies in parallel:

The first policy is to participate in projects through its companies by investing, purchasing, and marketing gas to ensure that it is a party to the production process and achieve economic profits. Moreover, Russia has already succeeded in achieving this, as displayed below:

The Russian company Soyuzneftegaz signed an agreement with the Syrian regime on December 20, 2013. The company was granted the right to explore and search in an area of about 850 nautical miles in the Syrian exclusive economic zone (EEZ) for 25 years (Karagiannis, 2014). Moreover, in early 2019, Russia signed another agreement with the Syrian government that gives Russia the full right to development and production in the Syrian oil and gas sector near Tadmur in the Homs governorate.

In addition, Russia has activated the NEFTEK Company in Lebanon since 2013 in the exploration of the economic zone. The NEFTEK Company is part of a consortium of companies that includes the Italian company Eni and the French company Total (Al-Ghannam, 2022). Also, between 2014 and 2015, Russian companies discussed with the Palestinian Authority possible options for cooperation in the oil and gas field; and the two sides discussed Russia's development of the Gaza marine gas field in September 2015. However, due to Israel's continuous opposition, no clear implementation formula was reached. Moreover, in February 2013, Gazprom attempted to strike a deal with Israel to exclusively buy liquefied gas from the Tamar and Dalit gas fields for 20 years and to market it. Despite Delek's willingness however, the agreement did not take place, as its American partner – Noble Energy – preferred the entry of a western party instead of the Russian one, represented by the Australian Woodside energy company (Karagiannis, 2014).

Furthermore, in December 2016, the Russian company Rosneft acquired a 30% stake in the Shorouk concession for the Zohr gas field, with a value of $2.8 billion. Moreover, the company owns 15% of the operating company for the privilege (Al-Ghannam, 2022).

The Russian second policy ensures that gas transportation projects from the Eastern Mediterranean are only implemented with Russia being a party to it. This is evident from the nature of the Russian position towards both the Syrian crisis and the Cypriot problem. The Russian support for the Syrian regime is largely linked to Russia's keenness that Syria not become a party to the western gas pipeline projects that compete with or harm Russian economic interests, such as the Qatari gas pipeline project, which was rejected by the Syrian regime.

Correspondingly, the Russian position on the unsolved problem of Cyprus represented the relative siding of Cyprus at the expense of Turkey and the assertion that Cyprus has the right to explore for and exploit natural gas as long as it is within its region. This is due to Russia's desire for Turkey not to have power over Cypriot gas, which would allow it to reduce its dependence on Russian gas (Stivachtis, 2021).

*5.2.1.2. Russia and Its Naval Military Presence in the Eastern Mediterranean*
In general, except for the time that followed the collapse of the Soviet Union, Russia has had a naval presence in the Eastern Mediterranean since the 1960s. In 2007, Russian naval forces gradually returned to the area, and since then, their presence in the Eastern Mediterranean has enlarged due to two factors:

The first is the de-committing of the American Sixth Fleet in the Mediterranean Sea significantly from what it was at the time of the Cold War; and the second reason is President Bashar al-Assad's call for Russia to intervene militarily in 2015, to help the regime and restore civilian and military control in Syria as a whole.

Russia took advantage of this circumstance and established a constant military presence in the Eastern Mediterranean, where it owns convoy ship No. 29, which was present during the Cold War, and the Fifth Operations Squadron, as well as the Russian military forces at the "Tartus naval bases" and "Khmeimim air bases," which have become focal points for the Russian military deployment in the Eastern Mediterranean, which the EU sees it as a dangerous penetration that threatens some European countries in the southern Mediterranean borders. The total number of Russian naval forces in the Eastern Mediterranean in 2022 includes 16 ships, 3 naval helicopters, and an aircraft carrier; clearly indicating Russia's full readiness to face any threats to its interests in the region (USNI News, 2022).

Through this policy, Russia succeeded amidst gas-related interactions in the Eastern Mediterranean, relatively due to its presence of heavy naval concentration in the region. It also succeeded in diverting the US focus from the Ukrainian crisis which is considered at the strategic depth of Russia – to focus on Syria, which is located in a clash area between the two countries.

Moreover, it overcame a significant strategic challenge: needing a Russian fleet for free access to the Mediterranean. Russia's access to the Mediterranean depends on passing through the Bosphorus and Dardanelles straits, which are under the control of Turkey. At the same time, with the Russia's involvement in exploration operations in the Eastern Mediterranean, there is a legitimate reason for the presence of Russian naval vessels on periodic missions in the region to defend gas platforms (Rettig et al., 2020).

On the other hand, the Russian naval presence in the Eastern Mediterranean also reflects a Russian strategy described as "Crawling Maritime Annexation," a strategy consisting of three phases:

In the first stage, Russian naval vessels accompany the drilling rig in the exclusive economic waters of the country that issued the permit. The second phase begins with the sudden emergence of a threat to the security of the platform, and here the Russian naval presence becomes permanent. The third stage will be with the beginning of gas extraction, as the host country becomes dependent on Russian companies to deliver gas production to ensure its protection. This explains the refusal of Noble Energy to sell a share of the Leviathan field to Russian corporations so that such a scenario does not occur with Israel as the strategic ally of the United States in the region (USNI News, 2022).

## 5.3. European Union and the Eastern Mediterranean Hydrocarbon Issue

Oil consumption contributes to 43% of the EU's overall energy consumption, with natural gas coming in second with 24%. The EU is the second-largest energy user in the world. Comparatively, only 2% of the world's natural gas reserves are owned by member states. The most significant proportion of gas exports to Europe comes from Russia; and the European dependence on Russian gas has reached such an extent that in 2015, the proportion of Russian gas exports exceeded 55% (Al-Ghannam, 2022), and 40% in 2022 of the total gas trade in the European Union (BBC, 2022).

This issue worries European countries and puts in the priorities of European energy security the necessity of diversifying natural gas sources to reduce dependence on Russia. There is almost unanimity among the governments of member states on this matter. The two leaders in this approach are France and Italy; particularly after the gas crisis between Russia and Ukraine in late 2005 and the beginning of 2006, after Russia cut off gas supplies to Ukraine and used it as a pressure card to achieve political goals (Karagiannis, 2014).

The series of hydrocarbon discoveries in the Eastern Mediterranean came as one of the possible alternatives to reduce dependence on Russia; especially since the European Union is directly linked to regional affairs in the Eastern Mediterranean, given that Greece and Cyprus are members of the EU and Turkey is also a candidate country for accession and a signatory to a customs union agreement with Brussels.

In addition to the fact that the European Union enjoys close relations with all Mediterranean countries within the framework of the Euro-Mediterranean Partnership (EMP) Program, it strengthened the European Union's idea of the vital role that the region will play in gas supplies to it and even to Europe. Hence, the Eastern Mediterranean qualified to serve as the third gas corridor. The first is Eastern Europe, which comes with Russian gas. The second is Southeast Europe, and the third is Azerbaijani gas (Alpago & Kılınç, 2021).

Accordingly, European corporations have been active in gas exploration operations in the Eastern Mediterranean countries; especially in Egypt, Cyprus, and Palestine, where there are prominent participations from several companies, the most important of which are British Gas, the Italian company Eni, the French company Total, and the Dutch company Shell. In Egypt, Eni witnessed booms in its activity between 2015 and 2017, especially after discovering the Zohr field in the Shorouk concession area. In Cyprus, vast parts of the exclusive economic zone of Cyprus were allocated to oil and gas companies from the Netherlands, Italy, and France. It is noticeable that European investments were limited to Israeli gas, so European companies focused on Egyptian and Cypriot gas, while Israeli gas was left to American companies (Al-Ghannam, 2022).

In addition to that, in January 2023, the Italian Eni company and the US major energy corporation Chevron announced that they discovered a new bed of natural gas in the Egypt offshore. The 1,800 sq km Nargis offshore area concession is operated by Chevron with a 45 percent share, with Tharwa Petroleum of Egypt owning the remaining 10%, while Eni maintains a 45% interest in the concession (Reuters, 2023).

Substantially, not all European Union countries agree on the importance of the Eastern Mediterranean gas as an alternative source to Russian gas. Germany, for example, does not attach importance to reducing dependence on Russian gas exports; but instead expands the volume of these exports through an agreement with Russia to establish an additional gas pipeline, which connects Russia and Germany directly across the Baltic Sea. This led to a split opinion within the European Union between France and Italy on the one hand and Germany on the other (Al-Ghannam, 2022).

### 5.3.1. NATO and the Suspended Problems in the Mediterranean Basin

The geopolitical balance among the Mediterranean's flanks (Northern, Central, and Southeastern Europe); the specialty of the history, geography, cultural, and security environment of the Mediterranean landscape; and the series of events after the Cold War all together contributed to complicating the NATO's policy in the region. Nevertheless, NATO's attention was drawn towards the Mediterranean region as far back as the 60s when the Expert Working Group on the Middle East and the Maghreb was formed. That notwithstanding, at that time, NATO's policy towards the Mediterranean remained mild until after the Cold War.

Hence, NATO's Mediterranean Dialogue was formed in December 1994. The inclusive goal of the Mediterranean Dialogue is to provide peace and stability in the region, bring out a better common understanding, and dismiss any misapprehension regarding the NATO's role in participating countries. The partnership and dialogue between the European and non-European countries in the Mediterranean Sea is a flexible and typical forum which has continuously progressed over the years to respond to regional changes. The Mediterranean matters for the European Union and the NATO's Mediterranean Dialogue were recognized as an integral factor of the NATO's cooperative convergence to security (Brandsma, 2019). So, it is time to ask whether NATO has fulfilled any of its responsibilities in the Mediterranean.

Indeed, from early 2010, the Middle East and Eastern Mediterranean region was marked by political turbulences; and the threats peaked in Syria, Iraq, and Libya. This progress gave rise to a tremendous migratory crisis and humanitarian disaster for Europe and brought a new international security threat. Hereafter, the Mediterranean is a place where NATO faced numerous questions. Ongoing conflicts in Iraq and Afghanistan, the war in Syria, the crash of Libya, the state deformation in the Middle East and North Africa, rising social inequality rate, pollution, and climate change are among the reasons that have contributed to a circumstance of durable chaos, which will be onerous for the alliance to protect at arm's length. Finally, the Mediterranean basin is a sensitive location where NATO's current and future role is vague and contested, both by its regional actors and members.

Although the European policy-makers and some elites viewed previously the chaos and threats coming from the Middle East and Southern Europe, the

Russia–Ukraine War proved that the devil is not asleep even in Europe. On the contrary, the Middle East and Eastern Mediterranean have the source of many opportunities, like exporting oil and natural gas in order to heat the European citizens, working in the industrial sectors, and decreasing the level of world economic inflation.

## 5.4. Intertwining International Actors in the Eastern Mediterranean

In summary, the main pivotal international actors in the Eastern Mediterranean are the United States, the European Union, and Russia; each of them seeking to achieve their goals for implementing their national interests. The priorities of the US foreign policy in the region are primarily to maintain its economic interests. It includes promoting the investments of American energy corporations in the region and using the natural gas resources in the Eastern Mediterranean as one of the alternatives to diversify the sources of gas imports for its European partners to reduce dependence on Russia and working to link the interests of its allies in the region with each other; and this was demonstrated through several actions, for example in the US attempt to normalize Israeli–Turkey's bilateral relations, as well as its support for the Eastern Mediterranean Forum.

For the European Union, gas discoveries in the Eastern Mediterranean represented a close option for importing gas within the European goal to reduce dependence on Russia. In this regard, European companies have been active in the region on a large scale, and the European Union has played a political role in supporting Cyprus against Turkish various operations in the region.

For Russia, the gas reserves in the Eastern Mediterranean pose little threat to its trade with the European Union. However, it seeks to address any threat, even if limited. In this regard, Russia has chosen to participate in the region through Russian energy companies, has already concluded several agreements with the countries of the region, and has also worked to have a heavy military naval presence in the Eastern Mediterranean to ensure safe access to the Bosphorus and Dardanelles straits under the pretext of securing its exploration activities.

Thus, the Eastern Mediterranean region has seen an apparent conflict between the American and Russian interests. American policy seeks to make the Eastern Mediterranean a regional center for gas exports to Europe, competing with Russia and reducing European dependence on Russian gas exports. As for Russia, it is exploiting the presence of gas fields in the Eastern Mediterranean to justify its presence, as well as achieving its historic military goal of free access to warm waters in the Mediterranean, as it tries to stand before the American projects by attracting some of the necessary parties, led by Syria – to complete these projects. On the other hand, the European Union countries do not have a unified vision for the Eastern Mediterranean. France and Italy support importing gas from Cyprus, Israel, and Egypt; while Germany is expanding its import of Russian gas.

## 5.5. Theoretical Arguments on the Eastern Mediterranean Hydrocarbon Issue

An eyeshot of this remarkable phenomenon in the southern and eastern Mediterranean noted that the matter of hydrocarbons has brought most of the various parties together at a table, even forming a joint summit called the Eastern Mediterranean Gas Forum (EMGF). Each country meets at a specific geographical point and has common borders and interests. Moreover, each country involved in the energy issues has its agenda, such as Egypt, Israel, Cyprus, and Greece. Turkey is also in this zone but has yet to find its share. Other owned energy countries outside the Eastern Mediterranean seek to provide their security and economic and diplomatic interests in this equation, such as the United Arab Emirates and the Kurdistan Region of Iraq. At a higher level, the European Union, the United States, and Britain considered their existence strongly regarding military, diplomacy, and economic dimensions. Hydrocarbon is a common ground for cooperation and a new regional security system. However, simultaneously, the surface remains tension and regional conflict.

Therefore, examining the factors or mechanisms presented by the theories of international relations is necessary for the hydrocarbon competitions in the Eastern Mediterranean. It evaluates the extent to which each theory can explain who or what enables the interpretation of energy security from the neorealist, neoliberal institutionalism, and regional security complex theories. This part argues that among these theories, neorealism provides more possible mechanisms that can be understandable in the political economy of natural gas and oil in the Eastern Mediterranean.

### 5.5.1. Neorealist Perspective

Realists and neorealists focus on the readiness of powerful countries as unitary players. The assumption is that the state implements actions in the system. Therefore, all actions can only uphold oil and natural gas when the powerful states push them (Krasner, 1993). Threats on oil and gas resources, water delineations, renewable energy, and electrifications, for example, are assumed to be oriented and promoted by the most powerful states to administer some form of order in international systems. Kenneth Waltz, the father of the Neorealism School, pays more attention to powers and the reality of power relations as a prominent factor in international relations; structural realism, or "neorealism," is an approach to international relations that confirms the role of "power politics" in international relations, views conflict, and competition as the two main characteristics, and believes that cooperation has limited possibilities. According to Waltz, "competition" and "conflict" are at the core of international relations. Also, the distribution of power among countries and the existing anarchic state of international relations literature are considered the two main pillars of international politics. The absence of a higher authority to settle international conflicts is anarchy.

For this reason, neorealism is divided into offensive realism and defensive realism. In these two types, the reality of the regional and international systems is anarchy, and should anarchy come to happen? Because each country is struggling to gain more economic, political, military, and diplomatic power, this is true that causes anarchy. However, ultimately it will be the reason for embodying "security and stability." Therefore, the principle of this international chaos must be decentralized, which means that it should not be gathered power in one center or one specific point. The reality of offensive realism insists that the state must gain power and create this chaos to impose its dominance through power and provide security. Nevertheless, defensive realism confirms that this anarchy structure should encourage the state to protect the balance of power and security in a softer way (Behravesh, 2010, pp. 1–6).

Hence, since 2010, two significant events have occurred in the region; the Arab Uprising/Spring and the discovery of natural gas on the Eastern Mediterranean coast. Since then, Russia militarily intervened on the eastern border of the Mediterranean Sea for the first time, they have air and ground interventions in Syria, thus preventing Assad's regime from falling. Then in finding and producing natural gas in Cyprus and Israel, the United States, British, and French interventions have increased much more in the region.

Essentially, the turmoil in the Mediterranean region as a series of events refers to the existence of conflict and chaos. The natural gas issue has created trilateral relations between Cyprus, Israel, and Greece; and more broadly, the EMGF has been formed. The conflict between Lebanon and Israel, Iranian intervention in the region, the continuing crisis in Syria, the Israeli-Palestinian conflict, the threats of the Iraqi central government and Iran on the semi-autonomous Kurdistan Region's energy pipeline, migrants crossing from the MENA countries to European countries; all of these phenomena have shown that conflicts are more than cooperation, and the distribution of power and struggle to gain much of economic, political and military hegemony by regional forces have formed "anarchy" in the Mediterranean region. As well as the conflicts and competition on natural gas and oil continued in the Eastern Mediterranean basin until the breaking of the Russia–Ukraine war (2022), which created the international energy and fuel crisis.

It is possible to use the liberalism approach to analyze the Eastern Mediterranean hydrocarbon issue due to the great role of the multinational energy companies in the region and its influence in the production of natural gas and its supply as a strategic commodity in the global market, but finally the neo-realism theory has more priority for this subject, because still, the "state" is a more important actor and role-player in international relations, which draws policy instead of multinational corporations. Moreover, according to the neo-realism approach, the contemporary world has an anarchic character; states have sovereign units considered the most powerful actors in the international system; So; the distribution of power and capabilities among units is of the greatest importance in the system. Thus, the US administration and the US Department of State have been able to issue a decision to suspend the natural gas pipeline project in the Mediterranean Sea before the war in Ukraine began in 2022. Once again, it is the US agenda's role to take steps to reshape regional policy and build a joint energy club in the region.

### 5.5.2. Neoliberal Institutional Perspective

The neorealists emphasize the reduction of state intervention in finance and economic activities, deregulation of labor and financial market, free trade, globalization, and promotion of the role of international corporations. Thus, the state should focus on improving its economic and social welfare. For instance, there are significant differences between the economic and political strategies used during the Cold War era and those used following the context of globalization and the technological innovation and digitalization that have become prevalent across all industries, particularly in the fields of production and consumption, divergent in various respects. The economic and political interests of the nation change with time, but there is one thing that is constant throughout all eras. As such, social scientists working in domains like politics and economics, where various theories have been formed, attempt to explain these shifting relationships using the framework of these ideas.

On the other hand, neoliberal and neorealist perspectives are becoming increasingly prominent globally in terms of politics and economics. This fact holds for the issue in the Eastern Mediterranean. This issue typically results from disputes between Greece and Turkey. However, the stance of Greece in particular, encourages other actors like France to get involved in this issue.

Neoliberalism holds that governments are not independent entities and are not the only players in international affairs. Transnational interactions are just as significant as traditional intergovernmental relations. In addition to states, there are other powerful actors, such as large corporations, banks, or organizations of scientific experts. Political power struggles and procedures are a part of states and their existence. In the interdependence approach, an area of analysis is their interconnectedness. International partnerships are essential since the Eastern Mediterranean problem and other current issues call for global solutions (Alpago & Kılınç, 2021).

Also, under the neoliberal international economy, it is widely believed that natural resource reserves such as oil and gas are the key to economic power and that those who control them may control the globe. This strategy is now viewed in terms of both neoliberalism and neorealism. This strategy can be used to base strategies on the current Eastern Mediterranean crisis since it serves both economic and political purposes by infiltrating the area and redistributing the balance of power in the world in favor of its interests. This is because it possesses subsurface energy resources like oil and natural gas, and it would be more reasonable to attempt to explain it using neoliberal and neorealist theoretical perspectives.

### 5.5.3. Energy Securitization in the Eastern Mediterranean: What Does the Regional Security Complex (RSC) Theory Propose?

This theory assumes that the post-Cold War condition and the concentration of power in different multi polycentric have increased the role of regional powers and the importance of "regionalism" in the international relations literature.

Furthermore, the concept of security has moved out of the classical phase since the Cold War, and various concepts have become more complex and "securitized." Previously, the concept of security was associated with military conflicts and preventing the crossing of Soviet hegemony to the countries of the Middle East and North African countries. The post-Cold War period is regionally different; many issues in the Mediterranean basin have been securitized, such as economic security, environment, immigration, food, and energy can be examined in various ways. When there is energy, energy security must be maintained at the regional level because the global energy and fuel crises are derived from regional crises (Stivachtis, 2021).

According to Buzan and Wæver (2003), there must be a specific degree of security interdependence between neighboring or closely contiguous countries for a region to be considered a regional security complex (RSC). Such dependency in terms of security must be strong enough to establish them as a plainly linked set and set them apart from nearby security regions. Although it won't make it a member of that RSC, a foreign power can nonetheless enter it if it enters into a security alignment with the local states (Buzan & Wæver, 2003, pp. 47–48). By doing so, energy introduces a multiplier effect on the level of securitization in existing state relations, both in positive and negative directions:

Looking at the regional level, some countries or areas geographically do not fall directly on the Mediterranean Sea, such as the UAE, Iraq, and the Kurdistan Region of Iraq; but they have directly and indirectly been an essential part of Mediterranean politics. The UAE is a member of the EMGF and participates in energy negotiations. The Kurdistan Region also exports oil to the port of Ceyhan in the Mediterranean Sea through the pipeline. With the US support, the region will be protected from Iranian threats and pro-Iranian groups in Iraq, Syria, and Lebanon, since Iran and Russia enjoy the Western countries facing an energy crisis.

Finally, we conclude that the conditions in the Mediterranean are theatrical. Because the political, cultural, economic, military, and geographical location of each country in this basin is different, there are countries like Turkey that can deal with domestic and regional crises. However, Turkey is an essential player in terms of the political, geographical, and military issues in the Mediterranean. Still, it has faced a crisis of marginalization by the countries involved in energy issues in the region.

Chapter Six

# Environmental Crisis as a Common Ground: Is There Room for Climate Change Challenges in the Eastern Mediterranean Hydrocarbon Issue?

### Abstract

This chapter investigates the collective response to environmental hazards within the Mediterranean basin and the southeastern Mediterranean region, exploring the challenges posed to current energy transportation and economic policies. Despite the ecological significance of the Mediterranean Sea, it faces mounting human pressures and political conflicts, particularly in its eastern area, which threaten its ecological integrity. The chapter examines the extent of consensus and cooperation among Mediterranean states in addressing environmental degradation, considering the diverse interests at play, including economic, commercial, and environmental concerns. With a focus on countries such as Cyprus, Israel, Egypt, and Turkey, the chapter assesses the scope of cooperation in combating environmental degradation and safeguarding human security in the region amidst the backdrop of climate change and ecological challenges.

*Keywords*: Mediterranean basin; environmental hazards; oil and gas industry; climate change; human security

## 6.1. The Problems Linked to Human and Geographic Nature of the Mediterranean Region

Indeed, the Mediterranean Sea represents a unique geographical and geopolitical nexus, encompassing developed nations along its northern coasts, underdeveloped countries along its southern shores, and nations with distinctive circumstances in its eastern region. This semi-enclosed sea is shared by 23 countries spanning 3 continents: Africa, Asia, and Europe. Approximately 150 million people inhabit the Mediterranean coastlines, constituting a third of the total population of countries bordering the sea. Over the years, the population of Mediterranean-bordering countries in Asia and Africa has surged from 105 million in 1960 to 480 million in 2015. Many of these nations heavily rely on natural resources to meet their domestic needs and bolster their economies (Lange, 2020).

The countries of the Mediterranean basin are known in the population, especially the southern part of the Mediterranean, along with a group of social complications and internal and regional conflicts, in addition to the effects of the legitimate migration and the resort. Also, the misuse of irrigation projects and agriculture activities are all issues that directly or indirectly affect the environmental quality in the Mediterranean (Cramer & Guiot, 2018).

As indicated in Madani's (2021) research, the Mediterranean Sea is an important area for marine biodiversity and is characterized by a unique geographical position with islands. It is an oasis of biodiversity, containing 7.5% of the animal marine wealth and 18% of the marine plant wealth worldwide. However, it represents only 0.7% of the oceans and seas in the world, along with various climatic conditions, this biological and climatic diversity is threatened by regional and local changes, as the level of the Mediterranean Sea has risen by 1.1 mm per year since 2006 on average and by 3 mm per year. Since the year 2020, it is expected that the average sea level rise will increase even more, if the pace of global warming continues outside the limits of 1.5 degrees Celsius, as it is expected to reach 10 cm in southern Italy, for example, which means that there is a variation in the impact of the different Mediterranean countries. In other words, the Mediterranean is affected by the geographical conditions and the ecological nature which varies from one region to another (Madani, 2021).

According to Smith (2011), the per-capita in the northern Mediterranean basin's countries reaches "32"; i.e., they use up additional resources at a rate of "32" times that of the average person in America or Japan, which means that they generate waste at a rate "32" times greater than the average southern Mediterranean resident. The average northern Mediterranean resident generates in just two years an amount of waste equivalent to what the average southern Mediterranean resident could generate throughout his lifetime (Smith, 2011, pp. 27–28).

### *6.1.1. Problems Related to the Relationship Between the Countries in the Mediterranean*

Indeed, industrialized (Developed) countries, particularly Western countries, are responsible for global warming and our planet's destruction. Whether it is about the capitalist world system and asset accumulation, or regional struggles for more hegemony and power, the situation ultimately requires them to take on this challenge to stop environmental threats, which have coined the term "climate justice" as a reference to breaking activity businesses protected by political elites, multinational corporations, and their military regimes. This matter requires a new balance between the northern and southern parts of the earth on one side, and the Northern and Southern Mediterranean on the other: The developed industrialized countries such as the United States and the countries of the European Union (the states which are located to the north of Mediterranean), which covers only 20% of the world's population, have historically produced more than 70% of polluting emissions since the year 1850 (Madani, 2021).

The current consumption and production systems, that is, the excessive or savage capitalism, depend on fossil energies, which is the primary cause of the problems of pollution and global warming, and even the pollution of seas and ocean waters, including the Mediterranean Sea, given that the most complex pollutants which impact the marine life result from the spillage of petroleum and chemical substances in the Mediterranean Sea.

In addition, poor societies in various regions of the world, including the regions between the two shores of the Mediterranean, are exploited for the benefit of significant countries; given that it is not possible to separate the devastating effects on the environment from their effects on humans; which means that there must be environmental justice that is subject to the natural will of people, in order to establish a sustainable relationship considering the needs of the community and not the needs of the major powers – through the excessive exploitation of the industries responsible for a large proportion of the climate pollution resulting from the burning of fuel – even though studies confirm a dark future for the entire world (Cramer & Guiot, 2018).

Truthfully, the modern world as a whole is affected by climate change. To this end, it is clear that the global economic system and the principles of economic achievement must be modified by reducing fossil fuel burning, industrial emissions, means of transportation, maritime transportation, and agricultural activities. These are the main causes of pollution in the world.

Even the technologies that have been found to reduce pollution take decades to mature and become practical, so technological development in many areas of life does not offer quick technological solutions which can be applied to reduce pollution in the Mediterranean Sea and climate change in the region in general. The shift to a green economy and clean, environmentally friendly trade requires more than application technology.

Thus, the three reasons associated with climate change; the rise in atmospheric temperature, the reduction in precipitation, and the increase in population growth have led to immediate effects on the needs of the population in the Mediterranean countries; particularly the need for water resources in the eastern area, from the Mediterranean Sea in particular to the southern ones. Minimizing the devastating consequences of this change is not related to who should bear the most significant burden and who should take the initiative in restoring the climate within the relationship between the northern and southern parts of the Mediterranean "fossil fuels." At the same time, it does not seem that the South, including the countries of the southern shore of Mediterranean, is ready to abandon the same system in search of development similar to the North. Its vision of responsibility necessitates that the northern countries bear the responsibility of adapting and decreasing pollution first (Madani, 2021).

## 6.1.2. Human Security Concerns in the Mediterranean Region

According to "the preliminary assessment by the network of experts on climate and environmental change in the Mediterranean region" (2019), the environment and climate changes, as well as political, economic, and social instability, threaten human security in multiple forms. About 40% of the coastline in the Mediterranean basin has been constructed up, and a third of the population (about 150 million people) live around the sea. In addition to that, the infrastructure is close to the average sea level due to the lack of storms and the limited range of tides. The consequences of these changes are rising sea levels, storms, floods, erosion, and subsidence which significantly impact coastal cities, ports, coastal infrastructure, wetlands, and beaches in the Mediterranean region (MedECC, 2019).

As a result, around 15 megacities located on the ports, with a population of more than one million in 2005, are at risk of flooding due to increasing sea levels unless further adaptation measures are implemented. It is projected that Mediterranean cities will account for half of the world's 20 cities experiencing the most significant increase in average annual damage by 2050, taking into account the sea level rise scenarios and current adaptation measures (Smith, 2011).

As pointed out by MedECC (2019), the adaptive capacity of the south and east of the Mediterranean is generally lower than that of the northern regions due to a combination of economic and social reasons that make it particularly vulnerable to these negative effects. Areas exposed to severe risks are also located in the south and east of the Mediterranean, including Morocco, Algeria, Libya, Egypt, Palestine, and Syria. A rise in sea levels by one meter will impact approximately 41,500 square kilometers of land in North African countries, influencing no less than 73 million people, equivalent to 11% of the population. Accordingly, 37 cultural sites are in danger of flooding during the next 100 years (flooding with a 1% likelihood of occurrence per year) from the Mediterranean Sea coasts listed on the UNESCO SHW World Heritage List, according to a study of those sites. In all, 37 of the 49 sites in the Mediterranean basin's low-lying coastal zones are at risk of flooding over the next 100 years (MedECC, 2019).

Studies indicate that by the year 2100, the risk of floods could increase by 50% and the risk of erosion by 13% throughout the region. The increase in the salinity of groundwater resources in coastal areas is another consequence of climate change and human activities that threaten human security (Lange, 2020).

Furthermore, the coastal areas suffer from saltwater intrusion; which will also increase the rise in sea levels. For instance, in 2020, 30% of the lands in Egypt suffer from the risk of salinity, and some areas of the Mediterranean basin are also affected. Regarding social instability, conflicts, and migration, human security around the Mediterranean largely depends on the social and political situation, but it is also affected by environmental changes, since climate change generally causes a decline in the available natural or financial resources, which contributes to the exacerbation of conflicts and wars. In addition to the continuing Syrian civil war and its foreign interference after 2011, it is well known that social, environmental, and political changes that constitute one of the important causes of forced human migration to less vulnerable areas worldwide (MedECC, 2019).

### 6.1.3. How Oil and Gas Industry Affect the Climate Change in the Eastern Mediterranean?

Determining the genuine greenhouse gas contribution of oil and gas production in the Eastern Mediterranean necessitates a comprehensive examination of all facets of the drilling fields' lifecycle: from construction and extraction to refining, transportation, and eventual end use of the products. However, this task is inherently challenging due to its dependence on various factors such as extraction methods, the quality of the fossil fuel extracted, and its subsequent utilization.

According to research conducted by Benedetti (2020) and submitted to the Fletcher School at Tufts University, flaring, the process of burning excess unrefined hydrocarbons, is highly polluting at the point of combustion. Furthermore, the study highlights other environmentally impactful practices, such as obtaining oil from tar sands or gas from fracking, which are notably carbon intensive. Notably, in Norway, the prohibition of flaring by regulators resulted in a significant reduction in emissions during the extraction process, estimated at 43%.

Illustrating the variability in the lifecycle of fossil fuels, the same study from Stanford University indicates that in the realm of transportation, the production, transportation, and refining of crude oil into fuels like gasoline and diesel contribute to approximately 15–40% of the overall greenhouse gas emissions throughout the entire lifecycle of transport fuel. Therefore, not only does further extraction of fossil fuels in the Eastern Mediterranean Sea contribute to global emissions from the eventual utilization of these products worldwide, but it also increases the carbon footprint of individual countries due to the introduction of this offshore industry, posing challenges for them to meet their nationally determined contributions as outlined by the Paris Agreement on Climate Change. The study from Stanford also suggests that despite the considerable variation in the carbon footprint of oil production, the most averaged-out estimate stands at 10.3 g of $CO_2$ per megajoule of crude oil (Benedetti, 2020).

The rise in atmospheric methane ($CH_4$) and carbon dioxide ($CO_2$), two primary anthropogenic greenhouse gases, is predominantly attributed to fossil fuel sources. A more focused approach to measurements, particularly investigating both offshore and onshore extraction sites, will facilitate a deeper understanding of emission distribution within the region. As noted by Jean-Daniel et al. (2021), the Mediterranean countries and the Middle East collectively account for 6.8% and 5.6% of global $CO_2$ emissions, respectively. In the Eastern Mediterranean and Middle East (EMME) region, $CO_2$ emissions have escalated from 662 to 831 metric tons per year during the period 2009–2018, primarily propelled by fossil fuel consumption in Middle Eastern nations (Jean-Daniel et al., 2021). Both oil and gas exhibit varying levels of $CO_2$ emissions during combustion. Oil emits approximately 8–10 kilograms of $CO_2$ per gallon, or 30–37.8 kg per liter, while natural gas emits around 0.05 kg of $CO_2$ per cubic foot, or 1.775 kg of $CO_2$ per cubic meter. It is worth noting that despite natural gas appearing as a low-$CO_2$ alternative fuel, it generates substantial amounts of methane compared to other fuels, which possesses a significantly more potent greenhouse effect (about fourfold) than $CO_2$ (Benedetti, 2020).

On the other hand, The US Geological Survey (USGS) has estimated that the eastern Mediterranean holds vast reserves, estimating approximately 122 trillion cubic feet of gas and 1.7 billion barrels of oil. To contextualize this, the gas reserves alone equate to approximately 76 years of gas consumption in the European Union. Currently, in the Eastern Mediterranean region, only about 50 wells have been drilled in its ultradeep waters. The drilling operations primarily utilize semi-submersible rigs, with gas now being transported through pipelines to Egypt and Israel (Burdeau, 2020).

In the broader context of global geopolitics, the preference matrix for global powers and industrial magnates remains skewed toward ensuring national security and fostering a competitive edge in energy distribution. This was evident at the COP28 climate change summit in Dubai, held from December 1 to December 4, 2023, where 134 nations inked the UAE Declaration. The summit saw an assembly of over 70,000 participants, including government leaders from 200 countries and a congregation of decision-makers, scientists, experts, heads of state, and members of international bodies, engaging in earnest dialogues to unearth solutions and financial strategies for climate change initiatives. However, the two largest industrialized countries, the United States and China, have not yet participated. In his speech at COP-28, the UN Secretary-General made it clear that the world must stop using fossil fuels to save the planet (Mediterranean Institute for Regional Studies, 2023). However, we are facing the opposite consequence, which is the increased attention of the world's countries to the hydrocarbon industry, increasing the demand and use of oil and natural gas, which has dominated the price of fuel in the global energy market.

### 6.1.4. The EU and Its Response to the Environmental Catastrophe in the Mediterranean Region

Three European countries completely located on the Mediterranean Sea are Greece, Cyprus, and Malta; while four European countries touch the sea partially; France, Portugal, Italy, and Spain. In addition to that, the Mediterranean Sea is considered as the European Union's strategic gate to the MENA countries in dealing with them in terms of migration, human trafficking, violence, and extremism, as well as transporting oil and natural gas from the MENA region to western countries (Holland, 2015).

Environmental issues affect the whole planet; so global warming, climate change, pollution, and food crises should not be confined to a specific region such as the Eastern Mediterranean.

After China and the United States, the European Union is the world's third largest polluter, accounting for 12% of total greenhouse gas emissions. It necessitates decreasing the rate of global warming by 2 degrees Celsius, which necessitates decreasing the planet's emissions of harmful gases to half or more by 2050, compared to the rate recorded in 1990, as the EU has embraced a "qualitative strategy" to achieve this goal, which is described as practical and executable, in addition to issuing more than 60 rules and laws on climate change (Ruseckas, 2022).

Climate change impacted Europe in the summers of 2021 and 2022 when it experienced the worst droughts in nearly five centuries and other issues affecting various sectors. In addition, Russia's operation in Ukraine and its various ramifications threaten European Union countries with a harsh winter, including the energy crisis, which might force them to resort to coal. Moreover, efforts to extract and produce more gas and oil in the world due to the energy crisis in Europe, then the food crisis in various parts of the world, the increase in the number of refugees due to the war in Russia and Ukraine, all together cause to pending the environmental issue in Europe and the world as whole.

Here, we see a paradox in the western countries' policies. On the one hand, they claim to protect the environment and solve the world's great problems, rising an amazing slogan and talking about lowering dependence on natural gas and oil, as the "Paris Climate Conference 2015." Developed countries make oversized promises at global summits every year to commit to solutions to environmental issues, but then nothing comes of it. As in the COP26 Glasgow Summit in 2021, they held the global summit to fulfill commitments (calling it COP27) in "Sharm El-Sheikh, Egypt," which took place in November 2022, in light of the EU's commitment to the need to reach better rates to protect the planet from the damage resulting from the matter of climate change, as it affects life itself, and to collaborate with the countries most impacted and most in need, to achieve the most global response to preserve the globe, which is now in a rising threat due to the issue of climate change. However, on the other hand, they work on increasing the production and import of oil and natural gas, intensifying conflicts over energy (Al-Sayed, 2022).

*6.1.4.1. The Possibility for Hydrogen Partnership in the Eastern Mediterranean and Europe*

Low-carbon hydrogen has arisen as a vital part of the EU's de-carbonization strategy. It also presents a new measurement of the EU's outward energy policy, given that a notable portion of Europe's future hydrogen requirements will have to be met through imports. In this context, the Eastern Mediterranean region stands out as a potential supplier of low-carbon hydrogen for Europe because of its closeness and large renewable energy potential. In recent years, energy cooperation in this region has focused on natural gas production. However, synergies could be realized if this cooperation expanded to hydrogen development for exports and domestic de-carbonization.

As Rau et al. (2022) argued, the non-EU countries of the Eastern Mediterranean basin, Syria, Lebanon, Jordan, Palestine, Turkey, and Israel have not been early movers regarding hydrogen; but to differing degrees, they have started to take note of the possible opportunities it presents. Aside from policymakers' general awareness of the hydrogen's growing prominence in the global energy and climate discussion, three key elements drive regional interest:

First, the EU policy prioritizes importing hydrogen from its southern neighbors; Tunisia, Morocco, Libya, Algeria, Egypt, Israel, Lebanon, Jordan, Palestine, and Syria; and its eastern neighbors; Ukraine, Moldova, Belarus, Georgia,

Azerbaijan, and Armenia; implying that the EU funding and policy aid could underpin the development of low-carbon hydrogen in the Eastern Mediterranean.

Second, many of the Eastern Mediterranean states are well-positioned to produce low-carbon hydrogen because of their renewable energy prospect and significant natural gas resources.

Third, the EU's plan to implement a Carbon Border Adjustment Mechanism (CBAM) indicates that regional producers of energy-intensive goods pre-destined for Europe will need to manage their carbon intensity over time, incentivizing them to comprise low-carbon hydrogen into their manufacturing operations (Rau et al., 2022).

***6.1.4.1.1. Hydrogen Strategy in the Eastern Mediterranean.*** The premature recognition of the hydrogen strategy in the Eastern Mediterranean region emerged from Greece; which regarded the role of hydrogen in its "National Energy and Climate Plan" published in 2019. "The National Natural Gas System Operator of Greece (DESFA)" is vigorously interested in the EU hydrogen dialogue; most notably through its contribution in the European hydrogen backbone initiative. It is balanced to start building a dedicated hydrogen pipeline infrastructure within Greece. The country is ready to pass its domestic hydrogen legislation. Egypt has introduced hydrogen into its "Integrated Sustainable Energy Strategy" as a major priority which was triggered in the COP27, which Egypt hosted in November 2022 (Ruseckas, 2022).

Egyptian state energy corporations are actively examining green hydrogen projects with the private sector, including main European firms. Eni, a major Egyptian state partner in gas and oil production, has been exploring the feasibility of hydrogen production with the state-owned Egyptian Electricity Holding Company (EEHC) and Egyptian Natural Gas Holding Company (EGAS) since July 2021. In August 2021, the EEHC signed a Memorandum of Understanding (MoU) with Siemens as a leading manufacturer of electrolyzes for green hydrogen production to work together toward developing a "hydrogen-based industry with export capability." A group of international and local companies signed a separate MoU to produce green (low-carbon) ammonia at Ain Sokhna. There have also been reports that this group's members are talking with several potential partners regarding future green hydrogen development projects (Rau et al., 2022).

Other countries in the Eastern Mediterranean need to advance more in their hydrogen policy approaches. In December 2021, agreements were signed to develop the first Israeli green hydrogen pilot project. Israel also has several high-tech start-ups working on hydrogen technology. Also, Turkey has yet to develop a formal hydrogen strategy. However, several technical initiatives and commercial studies are currently underway, primarily driven by the private sector and the scientific community.

Since the Eastern Mediterranean's abundant natural gas resources remain untapped, using natural gas as the basis for hydrogen production may have particular appeal in the region. Egypt has long been a main producer of natural gas; and Israel has recently joined it as an exporter, starting with Jordan in 2017 and Egypt in 2020. Also, to secure the region's natural gas possibility, one or more extra-regional export options will need to be founded; utilizing a combination of pipelines and existing Egyptian or new liquefied natural gas (LNG) liquefaction infrastructure. One clear lesson from recent years is that major export projects take time to move forward, even when the regional partnership is strong. Solutions that enable more gas to be profitably monetized domestically or within the larger Eastern Mediterranean region continue to pique the interest of investors (Chondrogiannos, 2022).

In these circumstances, utilizing natural gas to generate blue hydrogen for export or domestic use could be an attractive choice. Apart from its natural gas reserves, the Eastern Mediterranean has two other advantages that could help it become a blue hydrogen producer: First, because much of the regional gas resources are concentrated in large fields, unit production costs would be relatively low by global standards, and supporting the economics of hydrogen production. The second benefit is linked to Egypt's Nile Delta's depleted sandstone reservoirs, which are potentially suitable for $CO_2$ sequestration and could facilitate the carbon capture and storage solutions required to decarbonize hydrogen from gas (Ruseckas, 2022).

Furthermore, the European climate policy has taken into consideration the ambitious goal for greenhouse gas emission decrease. As Chondrogiannos (2022) states, the "European Green Deal" aims for Europe to reach zero environmental neutrality by 2050. According to this plan, Europe will no longer depend on gas and oil for import or export. Moreover, Europe has responsibility for the surrounding region, such as the Mediterranean basin: Following the Cold War's end, the EU's hegemony in the Mediterranean region has grown. In 1999, Europe and the Mediterranean Sea countries signed the "Barcelona Declaration" agreement to promote peace, security, and prosperity and increase regional cooperation and coherence. They outlined another common agreement, the "Euro-Mediterranean Partnership," as later renamed the "Union for the Mediterranean" pact in 2008. The EU intervened in the Mediterranean region to maintain security and prosperity while promoting environmental plans. However, we experience political and security conflicts and new geopolitical games over energy instead of focusing on climate change as a threatening phenomenon (Chondrogiannos, 2022).

Finally, the hydrocarbon competition in the East Mediterranean is not an opportunity for environmental protection perceptibly. However, the Mediterranean basin countries; especially Greece, Cyprus, Turkey, Israel, and Egypt, see the natural gas issue as a sensitive and golden opportunity associated to national security to enhance their economic interests and acquire more power. European countries are fully aware of the environmental risks and are considering scientific solutions to the problem. However, the reality of political requirements has dictated that another act be performed.

# Conclusion

In 2010, energy giant corporations flocked to the Eastern Mediterranean as natural gas was discovered. For more than a decade, Noble Energy and Exxon Mobile, British Petroleum (BP), French Total, Italian Eni, Israeli Delek Drilling, and the German DEA have all together devoted their technical, economic, and diplomatic power in order to pursue their interests in the Eastern Mediterranean. Nevertheless, in March 2021, Israeli Delek Drilling sold 22% of its stake in the Tamar gas field to the UAE's Mubadala Petroleum for more than 1 billion dollars (Anadolu Agency, 2021). Did all these biggest energy corporations and dozens of other companies in the Eastern Mediterranean come to this region randomly and spontaneously? Is a 1,900-km natural gas pipeline named the "East-Med Project" that costs $7 billion and starts transferring natural gas from Cyprus and Israel to Greece and other countries in 2021 just a usual issue and has not been considered before?

The Eastern Mediterranean region is characterized by deep-rooted border conflicts between the region's countries; most notably the Cyprus conflict between the Turkish and Greek Cypriots, and the border conflict between Lebanon and Israel, as well as between Palestine and Israel. Since maritime borders are directly linked to land borders, gas discoveries have added new dimensions to these conflicts, including problems in the ownership rights of the fields. In addition, three Eastern Mediterranean countries, namely Turkey, Israel, and Syria, are yet to sign the United Nations Convention on the Law of the Sea. Therefore, concepts such as the exclusive economic zone and territorial sea are not recognized in these countries.

Gas discoveries in the Eastern Mediterranean led to new regional and counter-alliances. The region witnessed rapprochement between Egypt, Cyprus, and Greece; based on solid elements of the partnership between them and everyday interests, especially with the agreement of the three countries to reject Turkish policies in the Eastern Mediterranean. On the other hand, another partnership formed between Israel, Cyprus, and Greece, which led to an understanding and convergence between themselves in the energy field.

Egypt, Turkey, and Israel stand out as the primary regional powers in the Eastern Mediterranean, each vying to establish itself as a central hub for gas resources, leading to conflicting interests. Egypt has worked to sign agreements with Cyprus and Israel to import natural gas and convert it into liquefied gas using its unique factories in the region and re-exporting it to Europe. Turkey aims to disable any gas export projects in the Eastern Mediterranean to which it is not a party, through pressure with the Cyprus problem, threats, and strong statements toward its regional neighbors.

According to our scientific research, there are four significant challenges facing the political economy of hydrocarbons in the Eastern Mediterranean:

First: The Cyprus issue is a challenge between Turkey and the Republic of Cyprus. This is directly a matter between Turkey and Greece, as well as Turkey and the European Union. As a regional power, Turkey wants to become a distributor of energy from Russia, Iraq, and Israel and other energy hubs to Europe. Greece has one foot in Europe and the other in the Eastern culture. This problem has been a reason for Europe's continued punishment of Turkey from 2010 to 2023. However, the discoveries of gas have also been the main reason for Turkey's incursion in Cyprus and Greek territorial waters.

Second: The Arab–Israeli problem. Since 2020, within the framework of the Abraham Accords and project, Israel has normalized its relations with Saudi Arabia, the United Arab Emirates, Bahrain, Oman, and Turkey. In addition, it has strong ties with Jordan and Egypt. However, eventually, the Palestinian–Israeli conflict will continue.

Third: Another acute problem is Turkey's geopolitical position. Turkey is one of the major players in the Eastern Mediterranean. At the same time, Turkey's geographical location between the Black Sea and the Mediterranean Sea, as well as Turkey, is the common pillar between the Middle East and Europe. This has created a sensitive situation for Turkey and the regional security system. Therefore, Turkey should redefine its policy: Will it become a commercial state and restructure its relations based on economic interests, or will it frame its policy as a military priority and consider interference in its surroundings?

As the director of the French Research Center on Iraq, "Adel Bakawan" pointed out, the moment of the Arab world's revolutions at the end of 2010 was, at the same time, a time of reviewing and reforming President Erdoğan's Turkish foreign policy. In this reformation, Turkey's Justice and Development Party believed that a special and unique model was created that could be transferred to all the Middle Eastern countries and built forms of state and society on it.

This is similar to the early 1980s, when the architect of the Iranian Revolution and the first leader (*Rahbar*) of the Islamic Republic "Imam Khomeini" wanted to rebuild the Middle East on the same model as the Islamic Republic of Iran had been built. However, 12 years later, Imam Khomeini failed to transfer his revolution to other countries. President Erdoğan has also understood that he was not only unsuccessful in rebuilding the Middle East on the model of the Justice and Development Party (AKP); but that this policy made Turkey shift from living in a big country with a unique position in the world system to a marginalized state and even President Erdoğan from a global accumulator personality to an unwanted person (Bakawan, 2022).

Fourth: Another global and regional deadlock in the Eastern Mediterranean region is the "Syrian crisis" (2011). The outbreak of war in Syria gave Russia an excuse to access the Mediterranean. The interference of some regional and great powers such as Iran, Turkey, the UAE, Saudi Arabia, Russia, the United States, and France in Syria has also complicated the scene. The humanitarian disaster and the millions of Syrian refugees are intertwined with the energy issue. However, Russia's military presence in Syria has cost billions of dollars. Russia is trying to recover the money by exploiting oil and natural gas opportunities in northern Syria.

Finally, the challenges will remain in the Eastern Mediterranean. Moreover, the outbreak of war in Ukraine (2022) proved that the influence of natural gas and oil on international relations is very durable. So, this research determines two main scenarios for the future of hydrocarbon political economics and geopolitical changes in the Eastern Mediterranean:

The first scenario is to stop the East Mediterranean Natural Gas Pipeline Project. For that, on January 9, 2022, an informal letter from the US Department of State was sent to the special departments of energy issues at Greece, Cyprus, and Israel foreign ministries. In the letter, the US administration declared its support for the East Mediterranean Sea pipeline project, which has created regional tensions and requires additional gas reserves in the region used through electricity cables to produce and run the electricity project. As Henderson (2022) at the Washington Institute for Near East Policy states, this project does not match the West's environmental plans, except this is only a media claim. So Henderson believes that instead of transporting the Eastern Mediterranean gas to Europe, it should be used internally. In the Eastern Mediterranean, for example, Turkey is thirsty for energy, and if Israel's gas is sent to Turkey, regional and political tensions will decrease (Henderson, 2022).

The second scenario is that energy can always be seen as a common ground. The East Mediterranean project will become a more significant global energy bloc and replace Russia's energy to the West. As well as, the Mediterranean Sea is home to dozens of strategic ports and serves as a vital conduit for transporting oil and various other goods. Therefore, the strategy of maintaining security and expanding the Mediterranean basin is a strong scenario. For this purpose, the natural gas and oil of the Kurdistan Region of Iraq and northern Syria are heading to the east of the Mediterranean Sea (this only passes with the security risks of Iran and Russia). Moreover, another Gulf energy line may also reach the Mediterranean Sea on Syrian or Jordanian land. It is visible that only six months after the beginning of the Russo–Ukrainian War, the European Commission President Ursula von der Leyen declared loudly that the "EU seeks to strengthen gas cooperation with Israel in response to Russian blackmail." Thus, on June 15, 2022, the EU signed another agreement with Israel and Egypt to export gas to Europe (DW, 2022).

Finally, the Mediterranean Gas Project is strategically important for Europe, Britain, the US, and Israel. The fuel crisis in Europe and the United States has given way to high international economic inflation. The West is considering giving up its dependence on Russian energy imports. Therefore, the United States and its allies will not leave the region politically, militarily, or diplomatically. Because China, Russia, and Iran are taking more dominance of this gap. So that, sooner or later the western coalition needs to promote more of the Eastern

Mediterranean Gas Forum (EMGF); which is established in 2020 and includes Israel, Cyprus, Greece, Egypt, France, Italy, the Palestine Authority, and Jordan. Thus, each of Saudi Arabia, the UEA, and the Kurdistan Region of Iraq will likely become an official forum member.

Therefore, the findings of this study can help us to better understand the regional decision-making centers and experts on energy issues in the Eastern Mediterranean and the Middle East as to how to find a new mechanism for a broader regional cooperation system in that sensitive era. It is no exaggeration to say that this effort is the latest doctoral research on the political economy of hydrocarbon in the Eastern Mediterranean within the new emerging regional order due to the consequences of the Russo–Ukrainian War.

# References

Administration of Barack Obama. (2011, August 17). *Executive Order 13582 – Blocking property of the Government of Syria and Prohibiting Certain Transactions with Respect to Syria. DCPD-201100578.pdf* (govinfo.gov).

Ahmad, S. (2020). Russia's foreign policy towards Syria: A post Arab Spring study. *Strategy International Journal of Middle East Research, 2*(2), 15–24.

Ahren, R. (2012, April 22). Egypt and Israel say cancellation of gas supply deal is 'commercial', not 'political'. *Times of Israel* [Online]. Retrieved December 5, 2021, from https://www.timesofisrael.com/egypt-reportedly-cancels-gas-supply-deal-with-israel/

Aksoy, H. S., & Roll, S. (2021). *"SWP". A Thaw in Relations between Egypt and Turkey – Stiftung Wissenschaft und Politik* (swp-berlin.org).

Akyener, O. (2016). Future of Israel Gas Export up to 2050 & Turkey. *Energy Policy Turkey*, (2), 38–51.

Alaaldin, R. (2023). *The geopolitics of Iraqi Kurdistan's Gas Reserves: Challenges and prospects.* Analysis Paper: Middle East Council on Global Affairs.

Al-Bayati, M. A. (2018). "Geo-Political Approach: Leviathan and Gaza Marine Gas – Israel and Turkey are Major Energy Players in the Market", University of Baghdad. *Journal of US-China Public Administration, 15*(1), 21–33.

Al-Ghannam, R. A. (2022). *International and regional conflicts over natural gas in the Eastern Mediterranean (2009–2019).* [Master's thesis, Alexandria University]. [Translated from Arabic to English].

Alhurra. (2023). *Iraqi Kurdistan resumes oil exports via Turkey after it was suspended due to the earthquake.* [Translated from Arabic to English language]. Retrieved February 16, 2023, from www.alhurra.com/zlzal-trkya-wswrya/2023/02/08/

Alipour, H., Kayaman, R., & Ligay, E. (2011). Governance as a catalyst to sustainable tourism development: Evidence from North Cyprus. *Journal of Sustainable Development, 4*(5), 32. https://doi.org/10.5539/jsd.v4n5p32

Al-Monitor. (2020, March 19). *Egypt and Turkey's energy face-off in the Mediterranean.* The Pulse of the Middle East.

Alpago, H., & Kılınç, M. (2021, October). Examining the economic and political dimensions of the Eastern Mediterranean problem from a macroeconomic perspective within the framework of neorealism and neo-liberalism. *Florya Chronicles of Political Economy* – Year 7 Number 2, 128–129. https://doi.org/10.17932/IAU.FCPE.2015.010/fcpe_v07i2003

Al-Rodhan. (2014). The geopolitics of culture: Five substrates. *The Oxford University Politics Blog.* https://blog.politics.ox.ac.uk/geopolitics-culture-five-substrates/

Al-Sayed, M. H. (2022). *The role of regional organizations in facing the issue of climate change: The European Union as a model.* Suez University: Faculty of Politics and Economics. "Arab Democratic Center". [Translated from Arabic to English]. https://democraticac.de/?p=85644

Alsharhan, A. S. (2003). Petroleum geology and potential hydrocarbon plays in the Gulf of Suez rift basin, Egypt. *AAPG Bulletin, 87*(1), 143–180.

Alterman, J. B., Ruy, D., Conley, H. A., & Malka, H. (2018). *Restoring the eastern Mediterranean as a strategic U.S. Anchor.* Center for Strategic International Studies.

## References

Anadolu Agency. (2021). *Delek sells Israeli gas field stake to UAE's Mubadala for $1B*. https://www.aa.com.tr/en/energy/energy-projects/delek-to-sell-israeli-gas-field-stake-to-uaes-mubadala/32537

Anastasiades-Akinci: Second official meeting, announces CBMs | News. (2017). *Sigmalive.com*. Retrieved June 4, 2017, from http://www.sigmalive.com/en/news/politics/130181/anastasiadesakinci-second-official-meeting-announces-cbms

Antreasyan, A. (2013). Gas finds in the eastern Mediterranean: Gaza, Israel, and other conflicts. *Journal of Palestine Studies, 42*(3), 29–47.

Aoudé, I. G. (2019). Conflict over oil and gas in the Mediterranean: Israeli Expansionism in Lebanon. *Arab Studies Quarterly, 41*(1), 95–110.

Aresti, M. L. (2016). *Oil and gas revenue sharing in Iraq* (p. 8). Natural Resource Governance Institute.

Argus. (2022, December 22). *Iraq eyes 2023 start of southern gas capture projects*. Retrieved February 17, 2023, from https://www.argusmedia.com/en/news/2403383-iraq-eyes-2023-start-of-southern-gas-capture-projects

Arslan, M. I. (2020, May 5). *ENI, total energy firms postpone drilling in E. Med. Anadolu Ajansı*. https://www.aa.com.tr/en/economy/eni-total-energy-firms-postpone-drilling-in-e-med/1829733

Ashwarya, S. (2017). Israel's Mediterranean Gas Governance: Evolution of domestic regulations and emerging regional issues. *Asian Journal of Middle Eastern and Islamic Studies, 11*(4), 76–99.

Auzer, K. A. (2016). *Institutional design and capacity to enhance effective governance of Iraqi-Kurdistan's oil and gas wealth* (pp. 159–162). University of Warwick Press.

Aziz, S. (2022). *Can oil and gas become a turning point in the geopolitics of the Kurdistan Regional Government?* Rudaw Media Network. [Translated from Kurdish to English]. https://www.rudaw.net/sorani/opinion/25102022

Bacchetta, P., & Van Wincoop, E. (2004). A scapegoat model of exchange-rate fluctuations. *American Economic Review, 94*(2), 114–118.

Bakawan, A. (2022). *The new Turkey's President Erdogan*. Rudaw Media Network. [Translated from Kurdish to English]. https://www.rudaw.net/sorani/opinion/240320221

Baram, A. (2022). *Iraq at a crossroads: Kurdish energy competition with Iran*. Analysis Paper: Geopolitical Intelligence Service. https://www.gisreportsonline.com/r/kurdish-energy-competition-iran/

Bassist, R. (2020). *East-Med undersea pipeline project now ratified by Israel*. Al-Monitor: The Pulse of the Middle East.

Bauer, P. (2013). European–Mediterranean security and the Arab Spring: Changes and challenges. *Democracy and Security, 9*(1–2), 1–18.

Baumann, F. (2008, March). *Energy security as a multidimensional concept*. Center for Applied Policy Research, No. 1.

BBC. (2014). OPEC Oil Output Will Not Be Cut Even If Price Hits $20 – BBC News. *BBC News*. http://www.bbc.com/news/business-30585538

BBC. (2022). *The European Union is moving to reduce electricity consumption and impose exceptional taxes on energy companies*. [Translated from Arabic to English; September 14, 2022]. Retrieved February 9, 2023, from https://www.bbc.com/arabic/world-62904008

Behravesh, M. (2010). *Realism and neorealism: An investigative overview* (pp. 1–6). E-International Relations. ISSN: 2053-8626. https://www.e-ir.info/2010/12/19/realism-and-neorealism-an-investigative-overview/

Benedetti, M. S. (2020, October 5). *Offshore oil and gas drilling environmental and economic effects in the Eastern Mediterranean Sea*. [Fletcher MALD Capstone Project].

Beshay, Y., & Devaux, P. (2017). "Egypt: Bid to be a Regional hub", ECO Emerging, 2nd quarter, *BNP Paribas*. Etats-Unis (bnpparibas.com).

# References

Betts, A., & Collier, P. (2015). Help refugees help themselves: Let displaced Syrians join the labor market. *Foreign Affairs, 94*, 84.

Biamouridis, A., & Tsafos, N. (2015). *Financing gas projects in the Eastern Mediterranean*. German Marshall Fund of the United States.

Bilgic, A., & Pace, M. (2017). The European Union and refugees. A struggle over the fate of Europe. *Global Affairs, 3*(1), 89–97.

Bowlus, J. V. (2015). *Pipeline partners: Expanding and securing Iraq's future oil exports* (pp. 726–740). Global Relations Forum Young Academics Program Policy Paper Series No.2; publish of global forum.

BP Statistical Review of World Energy. (2019). 68th edition.

Brandsma. (2019). *NATO and the Mediterranean*. European Institute of the Mediterranean. NATO-and-the-Mediterranean.pdf (iemed.org).

Bregolat, E. (2018). Russia in the Mediterranean and in Europe. *IEMed. Mediterranean Yearbook*.

Burak, S., & Margat, J. (2016). Water management in the Mediterranean region: Concepts and policies. *Water Resources Management, 30*(15), 5779–5797. https://doi.org/10.1007/s11269-016-1389-4

Burdeau, C. (2020, August 20). Eastern Mediterranean turns into source of gas and conflict. *Courthouse news*. https://www.courthousenews.com/eastern-mediterranean-turns-into-source-of-gas-and-conflict/

Buzan, B., & Wæver, O. (2003). *Regions and powers*. Cambridge University Press.

Camprubí, L. (2020). 'No Longer an American Lake': Depth and Geopolitics in the Mediterranean. *Diplomatic History, 44*(3), 428–446.

Caswell, C., D'apote, S., & Flower, A. (2016). *LNG markets in transition: The great reconfiguration*. Oxford University Press.

Chevalier, C., & Officer, M. L. (2004). Governance in the Mediterranean Sea, legal regime, and prospects. *IUCN Centre for Mediterranean Cooperation, 25*.

Chomsky, N., & Papp, I. (2013). *Gaza in Crisis: Reflections on Israel's war against the Palestinians*. Haymarket Books.

Chondrogiannos, T. (2022). *The climate hypocrisy behind the East-Med pipeline*. Investigate Europe. Retrieved February 16, 2023, from https://www.investigate-europe.eu/en/2022/the-climate-hypocrisy-behind-the-eastmed-pipeline/

Christou, G. (2002). *The European Union and Cyprus: The power of attraction as a solution to the Cyprus issue*. JEMIE, i.

Clarke, C. P., Courtney, W., Martin, B., & McClintock, B. (2020). *Russia is eyeing the Mediterranean. The US and NATO must be prepared*. The RAND Bloc.

CNBC. (2022). *Israel and Lebanon reach historic agreement to resolve a long-running maritime border dispute*. https://www.cnbc.com/2022/10/11/historic-agreement-between-israel-and-lebanon-brokered.html

Cohen, S., & Boms, N. (2021). "Israel and Lebanon: A bridge over troubled waters?" Tel Aviv University. *The Moshe Dayan Center for Middle Eastern and African Studies, 15*(1–12).

Correlje, A., & Van der Linde, C. (2006). Energy supply security and geopolitics: A European perspective. *Energy Policy, 34*(5), 532–543.

Cousin, E. (2023). *Out of gas? Egypt's ambitions to become a regional gas hub are dwindling*. Aljazeera. https://www.aljazeera.com/news/2023/10/4/all-gassed-up-egypts-ambitions-to-become-a-regional-gas-hub-are-dwindling

Cox, M., & Stokes, D. (Eds.) (2018). *US foreign policy*. Oxford University Press.

Cramer, W., & Guiot, J. (2018). *Climate change and interconnected risks to sustainable development in the Mediterranean*, MEDEC, pdf. https://ufmsecretariat.org/wp-content/uploads/2018/12/UfM-Sectorial-Report-Risks-associated-to-climate

Cropley, A. J. (2019). *Introduction to qualitative research methods* (pp. 3–11). University of Hamburg, Latvia: Zinātne. https://doi.org/10.13140/RG.2.1.3095.6888

# References

Cropsey, S. (2015). *US Policy and the strategic relationship of Greece, Cyprus, and Israel: Power shifts in the Eastern Mediterranean*. Hudson Institute.

Cyprus Mail. (2017). *Shuttle Diplomacy for Eide, Akinci says Anastasiades setting conditions (Update 5)*. Retrieved June 4, 2017, from http://cyprus-mail.com/2017/05/17/shuttle-diplomacy-eide-leaders-fail-bridge-differences/

Daily Sabah. (2020, May 4). *Turkey intensifies Eastern Mediterranean drilling despite pandemics*. https://www.dailysabah.com/business/energy/turkey-intensifies-eastern-mediterranean-drilling-despite-pandemic

Daily Sabah. (2022). *KRG in Iraq to start energy exports to Turkey soon: PM Barzani*. https://www.dailysabah.com/business/energy/krg-in-iraq-to-start-energy-exports-to-turkey-soon-pm-barzani

Dalay, G. (2021). *Turkey, Europe, and the Eastern Mediterranean: Charting a Way Out of the Current Deadlock*. Brookings Doha Centre. Turkey-Europe-and-the-Eastern-Mediterranean.pdf (brookings.edu).

Dana Gas Official Statement. (2023). *Dana Gas announces increase in Kurdistan Region production*. https://www.danagas.com/media/press-releases#sec-7266

Jean-Daniel, P., Riandet, A., Bourtsoukidis, E., Delmotte, M., Berchet, A., Williams, J., Ernle, L., Tadic, I., Harder, H., & Lelieveld, J. (2021). Shipborne measurements of methane and carbon dioxide in the Middle East and Mediterranean areas and the contribution from oil and gas emissions. *European Geoscience Union (EGU)*, *21*(16).

Dargin. (2007). *Hydrocarbon development in the Iraqi Kurdistan Region Petroleum Sector* (pp. 139–149). Energy Exploration & Exploitation Press.

Das, H. J. (2020). Israel's gas diplomacy with Egypt. *Contemporary Review of the Middle East*, *7*(2), 215–233.

De Guttry, A. (1984). The delimitation of territorial waters in the Mediterranean Sea. *Syracuse Journal of International Law and Commerce*, *11*, 377.

Delanoë, I. (2014). *The Syrian Crisis: A challenge to the Black Sea Stability*. Centre for International and European Studies. [Policy brief, No. 2/2014]. CIESPolicyBrief02.pdf (khas.edu.tr).

Demir, & Tekir. (2017). Sharing energy resources of Eastern Mediterranean: Regional and global dynamics. *Economic and Environmental Studies (E&ES)*, *17*(4), 651–674. http://dx.doi.org/10.25167/ees.2017.44.2

Dewdney, J. C. (2021, August). Turkey | Location, Geography, People, Economy, Culture, & History | Britannica.

Dolson, J., Shann, M., Matbouly, S., & Hammouda, H. (2000). Egypt in the twenty-first century: Petroleum potential in offshore trends. *GeoArabia*, *6*(2), 211–219.

DW. (2020, January). EastMed gas Pipeline flowing full of troubling questions. *DW News*.

DW. (2022). *EU, Egypt, Israel sign gas deal to curb dependence on Russia*. https://www.dw.com/en/eu-signs-gas-deal-with-egypt-and-israel-to-curb-dependence-on-russia/a-62140940

Egypt Today. (2019). *Egypt's gas exports double to 4.5 bcm in 2019*.

Egypt Today. (2020, August 27). *Greek Parliament approves maritime demarcation agreement with Egypt*. https://www.egypttoday.com/Article/1/91341/Greek-parliament-approves-maritime-demarcation-agreement-with-Egypt

Ekman, A. (2018). *China in the Mediterranean: An emerging presence*.

El Tawil, N. (2020, August 27). Greek Parliament approves maritime demarcation agreement with Egypt. *Egypt Today*. https://www.egypttoday.com/Article/1/91341/Greek-parliament-approves-maritime-demarcation-agreement-with-Egypt

Ellinas, C., Roberts, J., & Tzimitras, H. (2016). *Report on hydrocarbon developments in the Eastern Mediterranean: The Case for Pragmatism*. Atlantic Council's Global Energy Center and Dinu Patriciu Eurasia Centre. ethz.ch

Environmental Defense Fund (EDF). (2020). *The true cost of carbon pollution*. https://www.edf.org/true-costcarbon-pollution

Eralp, D. U., & Beriker, N. (2005). Assessing the conflict resolution potential of the EU: The Cyprus conflict and accession negotiations. *Security Dialogue, 36*(2), 175–192.

Escribano, G. (2017). The political economy of energy in the Mediterranean. In *Routledge handbook of Mediterranean Politics* (pp. 232–243). Routledge.

EU Commission Quarterly Report. (2019). EU Commission Quarterly Report on European gas markets, *13*(3), europa.eu

Eurcativ. (2022, October 12). *EU hails Lebanon-Israel maritime border deal.* https://www.euractiv.com/section/global-europe/news/eu-hails-lebanon-israel-maritime-border-deal/

European Parliament. (2017). *Energy: A shaping factor for regional stability in the Eastern Mediterranean?* Directorate General for External Policies. europa.eu

Even, S., & Eran, O. (2014). The natural gas revolution in Israel. In *Strategic survey for Israel 2013-2014* (pp. 189–203). Institute for National Security Studies.

Fattouh, B., & El-Katiri, L. (2015). *Lebanon: The Next Eastern Mediterranean gas producer?* German Marshall Fund of the United States.

Feng, Y. E., & Reshef, M. (2016). The Eastern Mediterranean Messinian salt-depth imaging and velocity analysis considerations. *Petroleum Geoscience, 22*(4), 333–339.

Fischhendler, I. (2018). The use of intangible benefits for promoting contested policies: The case of geopolitical benefits and the Israeli gas policy. *Geopolitics, 23*(4), 929–953.

Fischhendler, I., & Nathan, D. (2014). In the name of energy security: The struggle over the exportation of Israeli natural gas. *Energy Policy, 70*, 152–162.

Fisseha, M. (2017). Syrian refugee crisis, from Turkey to European Union – Methods and challenges. *Jurnalul Practicilor Comunitare Pozitive, 17*(3), 34–57.

Fletcher, N. (2016). Oil Price Surges as OPEC and Non-OPEC members agree deal to cut output. *The Guardian.* https://www.theguardian.com/business/2016/dec/12/oil-price-surges-opec-non-opec-agree-deal-cut-output

Fossil Free. (2015). What Is Fossil Fuel Divestment? *Brooklyn: 350.org.* http://gofossilfree.org/what-is-fossil-fuel-divestment/

Fouskas, V. (2001). Reflections on the Cyprus Issue and the Turkish Invasions of 1974. *Mediterranean Quarterly, 12*(3), 98–127.

Frappi. (2016). *The Energy Factor: Oil and State building in Iraqi Kurdistan* (p. 91). researchGate. Retrieved August 30, 2021, from https://www.researchgate.net/publication/308777708_Oil_and_State_building_in_Iraqi_Kurdistan

Friedman, S. M. (2011). Three Mile Island, Chernobyl, and Fukushima: An analysis of traditional and new media coverage of nuclear accidents and radiation. *Bulletin of the Atomic Scientists, 67*(5), 55–65.

Gaiser, L., & Hribar, D. (2012). Euro-Mediterranean Region: Resurged geopolitical importance. *International Journal of Euro-Mediterranean Studies, 5*(1), 57–69.

Gavriella. (2020). Joint Declaration of the 8th Cyprus - Egypt - Greece Trilateral Summit. . in-cyprus.com (philenews.com).

Genel Energy. (2023). *Genel Energy Official Statement.* Retrieved August 3 2023, from https://genelenergy.com/operations/production/taq-taq/

Geo Expro. (2019). *Giant Gas Field Discovery offshore Cyprus.* GEO ExPro - Giant Gas Field Discovery Offshore Cyprus.

Geopolitical Futures. (2022). *What are the fundamentals of geopolitics?* Retrieved November, 30, 2023, from https://geopoliticalfutures.com/learn-with-gpf/what-are-the-fundamentals-of-geopolitics/

Gillespie, R. (2011). The Union for the Mediterranean: An intergovernmentalist challenge for the European Union? *JCMS: Journal of Common Market Studies, 49*(6), 1205–1225.

Gillespie, R. (2013). *Change and opportunities in the emerging Mediterranean.*

Giuffré, M. (2017). From Turkey to Libya: The EU migration partnership from bad to worse. *Eurojus. it, 20*.

Global Witness. (2021, May). *Hot Under the Collar*. Global Witness Briefing. https://www.globalwitness.org/en/campaigns/fossil-gas/hot-collar-eastmed/

Gray, C. W. (2012). *Petro capitalism in Iraqi Kurdistan: Leveraging oil and gas firms in Post-War Iraq*. [CMC Senior Theses. Paper 337].

Grigoriadis, I. N. (2014). Energy discoveries in the Eastern Mediterranean: Conflict or cooperation? *Middle East Policy*, *21*(3), 124–133.

Grigoriadis, I. N., & Belke, L. T. (2020). UNCLOS and the Delimitation of Maritime Zones in the Eastern Mediterranean. *Policy*.

Gulf Keystone Petroleum. (2023). *Official web of the Gulf KeyStone*. Retrieved March 8, 2023, from https://www.gulfkeystone.com/operations/

Gürel, A., & Cornu, L. L. (2013). *Turkey and Eastern Mediterranean Hydrocarbons*. Global Political Trends Center (GPOT Center), Istanbul Kültür University.

Gürel, A., Mullen, F., & Tzimitras, H. (2013). *The Cyprus hydrocarbons issue: Context, positions and future scenarios*. PCC REPORT 1/2013.

Haartz. (2022). *Turkey could attack 'All of a Sudden One Night' Erdogan Warns Greece*. Retrieved February 18, 2023, from https://www.haaretz.com/world-news/2022-09-06/ty-article/turkish-leader-repeats-veiled-threat-to-greece-over-feuds/00000183-1332-d5cb-adb3-33fff9a30000

Hasan, S. (2020, January 28). Why is gas-rich Egypt importing fuel from Israel? *TRT World*. trtworld.com

Healy, J. C., Sanford, J. R., Reeves, D. F., Dufrene, K. J., Haskell, P., Luyster, M. R., & Bariudin, V. (2012, January). Design, Installation, and Performance of Big Bore (9 5/8 in.) Completions: Mari-B Field, Offshore Israel. In *SPE International symposium and exhibition on formation damage control*. Society of Petroleum Engineers.

Henderson, S. (2019, November). Israel's Gas Export Route to Egypt Finalized. *The Washington Institute for Near East Policy*.

Heshmati, & Auzer. (2019). *The role of natural resources in Kurdistan Regional Government's Economic Development*. Retrieved March 8, 2021, from https://journals.ukh.edu.krd/index.php/ukhjss/article/view/31/92

Hilali. (2016). Geopolitics of Syrian crisis and future of Alawite Heartland. *Margalla Papers*. 5_Dr_A_Z_Hilali.pdf (ndu.edu.pk).

Hindu Times. (2021, February). Israel, Egypt may build gas pipe as they eye European market. *Hindu Times*.

Högselius, P. (2018). *Energy and geopolitics*. Routledge. ISBN 9781138038394.

Holland, A. (2015). *Energy and geopolitics in the Eastern Mediterranean*. American Security Project.

Holtug, N. (2016). A fair distribution of refugees in the European Union. *Journal of Global Ethics*, *12*(3), 279–288.

Inbar, E. (2014). *The new strategic equation in the Eastern Mediterranean*. Begin-Sadat Center for Strategic Studies, Bar-Ilan University.

Inbar, E. (2022). What is the agenda for the Eastern Mediterranean? Ekathimerini. https://www.ekathimerini.com/opinion/1188713/what-is-the-agenda-for-the-eastern-mediterranean/

Institut Montaigne. (2020). *Whose sea? A Greek international law perspective on the Greek-Turkish disputes*. Institut Montaigne. https://www.institutmontaigne.org/en/blog/whose-sea-greek-international-law-perspective-greek-turkish-disputes

International Crisis Group. (2012, April 2). *Aphrodite's gift: Can Cypriot gas power a new dialogue?* Crisis Group Europe Report N°216.

International Energy Agency. (2020). *Global $CO_2$ emissions in 2019*. Retrieved February 12, 2023, from https://www.iea.org/articles/global-co2-emissions-in-2019

International Energy Agency. (2023). *Global gas demand set for stronger growth in 2024 despite heightened geopolitical uncertainty*. Retrieved January 26, 2024, from https://www.iea.org/news/global-gas-demand-set-for-stronger-growth-in-2024-despite-heightened-geopolitical-uncertainty

Iraqi Constitution of 2005. (2023). Retrieved February 17, 2023, from constituteproject.org

Ismael, H. M. (2018). *The geopolitical challenge of Iraqi Kurdistan's natural gas* (pp. 81–82). University of North Carolina at Greensboro.

Ismael, H. M. (2020). Kurdistan's role in European energy security. *Journal of Geography, Politics and Society*, 33–34.

Ismail, M. S., Moghavvemi, M., & Mahlia, T. M. I. (2013). Energy trends in Palestinian territories of West Bank and Gaza Strip: Possibilities for reducing the reliance on external energy sources. *Renewable and Sustainable Energy Reviews, 28*, 117–129.

Israeli Ministry of Energy. (2020). *Another step towards the EastMed pipeline*. Energy-sea.gov.il

Jüde. (2017). *Contesting borders? The formation of Iraqi Kurdistan's de facto state* (pp. 847–848). Oxford University Press.

Kader, & Lecha, E. S. (2018). *Iraqi Kurdistan and beyond: The EU's stakes* (pp. 3–4). Retrieved August 30, 2021, from https://www.iai.it/en/pubblicazioni/iraqi-kurdistan-and-beyond-eus-stakes)

Kalkan, E. (2020). The Longstanding Dispute between Turkey and Greece: The Aegean Issue. *Uluslararası İktisadi ve İdari İncelemeler Dergisi*, (28), 167–174.

Kamal. (2018). *Oil & Gas Industry of Kurdistan Region of Iraq: Challenges and opportunities* (pp. 1–2). Crimson.

Karagiannis, E. (2014). *The Emerging Gas Region of the Eastern Mediterranean: Global and regional powers in a changing world*. FIACSI- ISA Joint International Conference, Buenos Aires.

Karim, S. (2016, April). Syrian crisis: Geopolitics and implications. *BIISS Journal, 37*(2), 107–132.

Kaye, S. B. (2017). *The law of the sea convention and sea level rise in light of the South China Sea Arbitration*.

Keohane, R. O., & Nye, J. S. (1977). *Power and interdependence*.

Khadduri, W. (2012). East Mediterranean gas: Opportunities and challenges. *Mediterranean Politics, 17*(1), 111–117.

Klich. (2013). Dependent yet defiant: The implications of unilateralism in Iraqi Kurdistan. *The ANU Undergraduate Research Journal, 5*, 61–68.

Knell, Y. (2013, May). Gas finds in east Mediterranean may change strategic balance. *BBC News*.

Knights. (2010). *The Washington Institute for Near East Policy*. Iraq-Turkey Pipeline Arbitration: Avoiding a Policy Train Wreck | The Washington Institute.

Kontos, M. (2018). Power games in the exclusive economic zone of the Republic of Cyprus: The Trouble with Turkey's Coercive Diplomacy. *The Cyprus Review, 30*(1), 51–70.

Korkut, E. (2017). Turkey and the International Law of the Sea. *SJD Dissertations, 5*. https://elibrary.law.psu.edu/sjd/5

Kostianoy, A. G., & Carpenter, A. (2018). Oil and gas exploration and production in the Mediterranean Sea. In *Oil pollution in the Mediterranean Sea: Part I*. https://doi.org/10.1007/698_2018_373

Kozma, T. (2020). *Turkey and the geopolitics of natural gas in the Eastern Mediterranean*. Trends Research and Advisory.

Kraemer. (2019). *The Iraq-Turkey pipeline dispute: Opportunity in arbitration*. Retrieved August 25, 2021, from https://www.justsecurity.org/65893/the-iraq-turkey-pipeline-dispute-opportunity-in-an-arbitration/

Krasner, S. D. (1993). Sovereignty, regimes, and human rights. *Regime Theory and International Relations*, 139–167.

## References

Krhovska, H. (2014). *Conflict Resolution in the disputes over Resources in the Eastern Mediterranean: The Case of Israel and Lebanon*. [Master's Thesis, Masaryk University, Faculty of Social Studies, Political Science Department].

Kukushkin, V. (2021). Syria and hydrocarbons: Present and prospective politico-economic issues. In *The Syrian crisis* (pp. 161–178). Springer.

Kumar, D. K. (2020, September 2). Feature: 'Cyprus eyes progress on Aphrodite gas development, pipeline plan'. *Reuters News*. spglobal.com

Kurdistan Regional Government. (2023). Retrieved February 17, 2023, from https://gov.krd/english/government/the-prime-minister/activities/posts/2023/february/prime-minister-masrour-barzani-to-attend-world-government-summit-2023/

La Jeunesse, I., Cirelli, C., Aubin, D., Larrue, C., Sellami, H., Afifi, S., & Soddu, A. (2016). Is climate change a threat for water uses in the Mediterranean region? Results from a survey at local scale. *Science of the Total Environment, 543*, 981–996.

Lange, M. A. (2020). *Climate change in the Mediterranean; Environmental impacts and extreme events*. IEMed. The Cyprus Institute; Energy, Environment and Water Research Center. Retrieved December 11, 2023, from https://www.iemed.org/publication/climate-change-in-the-mediterranean-environmental-impacts-and-extreme-events/

Le Billon, P. (2004). The geopolitical economy of 'resource wars'. *Geopolitics, 9*(1), 1–28.

Legrenzi, M., & Momani, B. (Eds.) (2011). *Shifting geo-economic power of the Gulf: Oil, Finance and institutions*. Ashgate Publishing Ltd.

Lujala, & Rustad. (2011). High-value natural resources: A blessing or a curse for peace? *Sustainable Development Law & Policy, 12*(1), 20–21.

Madani, L. (2021). Environmental challenges in the Mediterranean between the country interest and the common interest: Algeria as an example. *Journal of North African Economics, 17*(26), 465–478. ISSN: 1112-6132.

Mamedov. (2021). Russia: Towards a balance of interest in the Mediterranean region. *Russian International Affairs Council*. russiancouncil.ru

Mamshae. (2020). *Kurdistan's democratic developments amid a rentier oil economy: A political economy approach* (pp. 69–71).

Marghelis, A. (2021). The maritime delimitation agreement between Greece and Italy of 9 June 2020: An analysis in the light of International Law, national interest and regional politics. *Marine Policy, 126*, 104403.

Masnadi, M. S., El-Houjeiri, H. M., Brandt, A. R., & Koomey, J. (2018). Global carbon intensity of crude oil production. *Science, 361*(6405), 851–853. https://doi.org/10.1126/science.aar6859

Masuda, T. (2007). Security of energy supply and the geopolitics of oil and gas pipelines. *European Review of Energy Markets, 2*(2), 1–32.

Mearsheimer, J., & Walt, S. (2006). *The Israel Lobby and US Foreign Policy* (pp. 3–4). University of Chicago, Harvard University. 'RWP06-011'.

MedECC. (2019). Preliminary assessment by the network of experts on climate and environmental change in the Mediterranean region – "2019 risks related to climate and environmental changes in the Mediterranean region".

Mediterranean Institute for Regional Studies. (2019). *Stubborn Kurdish Petroleum Resources: Surveying Actual data and investigating the declared Numbers*. [Policy Paper No. 69].

Mediterranean Institute for Regional Studies. (2022). *A perspective in order to protect energy security in the Kurdistan Region*. [Translated from Kurdish to English], pp. 1–14. https://www.mirs.co/KU/details.aspx?jimare=242

Mediterranean Institute for Regional Studies. (2022, December 29). *Energy geopolitics and conflict between energy basins: A perspective beside securitization of the new regional and global order*. [MIRS; Policy paper]. https://www.mirs.co/details.aspx?jimare=186

Mediterranean Institute for Regional Studies. (2023). *Analyzing Russia's Involvement in Iraq and the Kurdistan Region's Energy Sector*. [Policy paper]. https://www.mirs.co/details.aspx?jimare=230

Mills. (2016a). *Pipeline politics: Oil, economics, law, and politics in the KRI since 2005* (pp. 41–42). Oxford Institute for Energy Studies.

Mills. (2016b). *Under the mountains: Kurdish oil and regional politics* (pp. 1–17). Oxford Institute for Energy Studies.

Ministry of Foreign Affairs of the Hellenic Republic. (2014). *Egypt-Greece-Cyprus Trilateral Summit Cairo Declaration*. mfa.gr.

Mirza, M. N., Abbas, H., & Qaisrani, I. (2021). Anatomising Syrian crisis: Enumerating actors, motivations, and their strategies (2011-2019). *Liberal Arts and Social Sciences International Journal, 5*(1), 41–54.

Mohammed, H. J., Schrock, S., & Jaff, D. (2019, August). The challenges impeding traffic safety improvements in the Kurdistan Region of Iraq. *Transportation Research Interdisciplinary Perspectives*. https://doi.org/10.1016/j.trip.2019.100029

Moon, C. W., & Lado, A. A. (2000). MNC-host government bargaining power relationship: A critique and extension within the resource-based view. *Journal of Management, 26*(1), 85–117.

Moore, S. (2013). Envisioning the social and political dynamics of energy transitions: sustainable energy for the Mediterranean region. *Science as Culture, 22*(2), 181–188.

Motarzavi. (2019). How Russia is filling the gap left by Trump's withdrawal of US troops from Syria. Independent News.

Nakhle, C. (2023). Egypt's gas exports under threat. *Crystol Energy*. https://www.crystolenergy.com/egypts-gas-exports-under-threat/

Natali. (2014). [online] *Turkey's Kurdish oil gamble – Al-Monitor: The Pulse of the Middle East*.

Nathanson, R., & Levy, R. (2012). *Natural Gas in the Eastern Mediterranean: Casus belli or chance for regional cooperation* (pp. 58–62). Institute for National Security Studies, Tel Aviv.

NS Energy. (2021). *Eastern Mediterranean Pipeline Project*. nsenergybusiness.com

Nugent, N. (2010). *The government and politics of the European Union*. Palgrave Macmillan.

Okumuş, O. (2020). *Value Beyond Price: Prioritizing political stability and regional integration when financing Eastern Mediterranean Gas, Atlantic council in Turkey*. Value-Beyond-Price-OO.pdf (atlanticcouncil.org).

Olgun, M. E. (2019). *Hydrocarbons will determine the political future of Cyprus*. [IAI Papers 19].

Özden, S. (2013). *Syrian refugees in Turkey*. European University Institute. Migration Policy Center.

Özgür, H. K. (2017). Eastern Mediterranean Hydrocarbons: Regional potential challenges ahead, and the 'hydrocarbonization' of the Cyprus problem. *Perceptions: Journal of International Affairs, 22*(2), 31–56.

Paasche, & Mansurbeg. (2014). Kurdistan Regional Government-Turkish Energy Relations: A complex partnership. *Eurasian Geography and Economics, 55*, 2–3.

Palacios, X. (2018). *Conflict in Cyprus: Religion, ethnicity and natural gas pipelines* IEEE. ES. Opinion Document 90/2018.

Palani, K., Khidir, J., Dechesne, M., & Bakker, E. (2021). Strategies to gain international recognition: Iraqi Kurdistan's September 2017 Referendum for Independence. *Ethnopolitics, 20*(4), 406–427. https://doi.org/10.1080/17449057.2019.1596467

Panayiotides, N. (2013). The new geopolitics of the natural gas in the levant. *Palestine-Israel Journal of Politics, Economics, and Culture, 19*(1/2), 154.

Parlar Dal, E. (2016). Impact of the Trans-nationalization of the Syrian Civil War on Turkey: Conflict spillover cases of ISIS and PYD-YPG/PKK. *Cambridge Review of International Affairs, 29*(4), 1396–1420.

## References

Pericleous, C. (2012). Cyprus: A last window of opportunity? Natural gas revives solution dynamic. *Insight Turkey, 14*(1), 93.

Perrin, F. (2017). The North African gas export outlook between commercial and political challenges. In *The European gas markets* (pp. 281–302). Palgrave Macmillan.

Petoil Official Web. (2023). *A brief history of Pet holding*. Retrieved August 3, 2023, from https://www.petoil.com.tr/en/briefhistory.html

Poullikkas, A., Demokritou, P., Sourkounis, C., & Al-Assaf, Y. (2013). Power options for the Eastern Mediterranean Region. *Conference Papers in Energy*, 1–2. https://doi.org/10.1155/2013/487837

Prifti, B. (2017). *US foreign policy in the Middle East: The case for continuity*. Springer.

Raheb, M. (2002). Sailing through troubled waters: Palestinian Christians in the Holy Land. *Dialog, 41*(2), 97–102.

Ratner, M. (2011). *Israel's offshore natural gas discoveries enhance its economic and energy outlook*. CRS Report for Congress. energy-sea.gov.il

Ratner, M. (2016). *Natural gas discoveries in the Eastern Mediterranean, Congressional Research Service, R44591*.

Rau, M., Seufert, G., & Westphal, K. (2022). *The Eastern Mediterranean as a Focus for the EU's Energy Transition*. Stiftung Wissenschaft und Politik (SWP). https://doi.org/10.18449/2022C08

Reality Check Team. (2019, November). Syria war: Who benefits from its oil production? *BBC News*.

Reed, S. (2016). Russia and others join OPEC in rare, coordinated push to cut oil output. *The New York Times*, December 10. http://www.nytimes.com/2016/12/10/business/russia-opec-saudi-arabia-cut-oil-output.html

Reed, J. (2017, April). Israeli Signs Pipeline dealing push to export gas to Europe. *The Financial Times Limited*. ft.com

Rettig, E., Polinov, S., & Chorvel, S. (2020, June). 'What does Russia want with Lebanon's gas fields? *Jerusalem Post* Retrieved February 9, 2023, from https://www.jpost.com/opinion/what-does-russia-want-with-lebanons-gas-fields-630557

Reuters. (2021a). Turkey says it may negotiate maritime demarcation with Egypt. *Reuters News*.

Reuters. (2021b). Egypt aims to produce 7.2 billion cubic feet of natural gas per day in 2021/22. *Reuters News*.

Reuters. (2023). *Eni, Chevron announce the new gas discovery in Egyptian East Med field*. Retrieved September 2, 2023, from https://www.reuters.com/business/energy/eni-announces-new-gas-discovery-offshore-egypt-2023-01-15/

Roberts, J. (2016). *Iraqi Kurdistan oil and gas outlook* (pp. 7–2). Atlantic Council's Global Energy Center and Dinu Patriciu Eurasia Center.

Roberts, M. J. (2018). Turkey and the Kurdistan region of Iraq: Strained energy relations. *Turkish Policy Quarterly, 17*(3), 100.

Rogg, & Rimscha (2007, December). The Kurds as parties to and victims of conflicts in Iraq. *International Review on Red Cross, 89*(868), 8322–833.

Rosamond, B. (2000). *Theories of European integration*. The European Union Series, Palgrave. ISBN-10: 0312231202.

Rosenthal, G. G. (2013). *The Mediterranean Basin: Its political economy and changing international relations*. Elsevier.

Roucek, J. S. (1953). The Geopolitics of the Mediterranean, I. *The American Journal of Economics and Sociology, 12*(4), 347–354.

Rudaw. (2021). *SOMO: Kurdistan Region exports '430,000' barrels, and the 2021 budget obliges it to deliver 250,000 barrels*. [Translated from Arabic to English]. https://www.rudaw.net/arabic/kurdistan/020120218

Rudaw. (2022). *Deputy PM Talabani addresses Erbil-Baghdad issues at Greece economic forum*. https://www.rudaw.net/english/kurdistan/090420221

Rudaw. (2023). *Gas production in Kurdistan Region hits a new record.* Retrieved February 17, 2023, from https://www.rudaw.net/english/business/09112022#:~:text=Dana%20 Gas%20is%20currently%20implementing,US%20International%20Development %20Finance%20Corporation

Rühl, C. (2010). Global energy after the crisis: Prospects and priorities. *Foreign Affairs*, 63–75.

Ruseckas, L. (2022). *Europe and the Eastern Mediterranean: The potential for hydrogen partnership.* Stiftung Wissenschaft und Politik (SWP). https://doi.org/10.18449/2022c50v02

Salih, D. (2022). *IRGC: View of the relationship with Kurdistan Region.* Emirates Policy Center. https://epc.ae/en/details/featured/irgc-view-of-the-relationship-with-kurdistan-region

Salih, R. S., & Yamulki (2020). Reforms feasibility in Kurdistan Region Petroleum contracts triggered by the new regional blocks divisions. *International Journal of Business and Social Science*, *11*(5), 35–40.

Santis. (2003). *NATO's Agenda and the Mediterranean Dialogue.* https://doi.org/10.1007/978-3-642-55854-2_9

Schneider, B. H., Benenson, J., Fülöp, M., Berkics, M., & Sándor, M. (2014). *Cooperation and competition.*

Sergeyevna, A. E. (2020). Russia navigates complex competing interests in the Eastern Mediterranean. In M. Tanchum (Ed.), *Eastern Mediterranean in uncharted waters: Perspectives on emerging geopolitical realities* (pp. 52–58). Konrad-Adenauer-Stiftung.

Shaban, F. (2019). *The oil and natural gas conflict in Israel.* ORSAM-Center for Middle Eastern Studies.

Shafaq News. (2023, January 23). *Iraq announces the addition of 6 billion barrels of oil and 23 billion cubic feet to the national reserves.* [The source translated from Arabic to English]. Retrieved February 17, 2023, from https://shafaq.com/ar/%D8%A7%D9% 82%D8%AA%D8%B5%D9%80%D8%A7%

Shaffer, B. (2018). Eastern Mediterranean Energy: A decade after the major discoveries. *Turkish Policy Quarterly*, *17*(3), 89–97.

Shaltami, O. R. (2020). *1st International Conference on Geosciences (ICG2020) at the University of Nova Gorica, Slovenia: Eastern Mediterranean Gas: A Review.* researchgate.net

Shama, N. (2019). *Between alliance and entente: The Egyptian-Greek-Cypriot Partnership, Re-Imagining the Eastern Mediterranean Series: PCC REPORT 3/2019.*

ShaMaran Petroleum Report. (2023) *ShaMaran reports strong first quarter results.* Retrieved August 3, 2023, from https://shamaranpetroleum.com/news/shamaran-reports-strong-first-quarter-results-122840/

Smeeknens, D., & Keil, S. (2022). *The Iraqi Oil and Gas Dispute between Baghdad and Erbil: A Commentary on the Iraqi Federal Supreme Court Judgment of 15 February 2022* (pp. 4–11). [University of Fribourg, Institute of Federalism (IFF), working paper]. www.federalism.ch

Smith, L. C. (2011). *The World in 2050: Four forces shaping civilization's northern future.* [Translated from English to Arabic by Hassan Al-Bustani, Arab Scientific publisher, Beirut].

Sorenson. (2010). *Interpreting the Middle East (Essential Themes)* (p. 337). Westview Press Air War College.

Sözen, A., & Özersay, K. (2007). The Annan Plan: State succession or continuity. *Middle Eastern Studies*, *43*(1), 125–141.

Statista. (2024). *Demand for crude oil worldwide from 2005 to 2023, with a forecast for 2024.* Retrieved April 26, 2024, from https://www.statista.com/statistics/271823/globalcrude-oil-demand/

## References

Stauffer, T. R. (2004, March). [Online] *Pipeline or pipe dream? The Kirkuk-Haifa Scheme* (p. 21). Washington Report on Middle East Affairs (WRMEA).

Stergiou. (2012). *Russian Policy in the Eastern Mediterranean and The Implications for EU External Action*. European Union Institute for Security Studies (europa.eu).

Stevens, P. J. (2004). The prospects for oil prices: The dangers of wet barrel supply chasing paper barrel demand. *Oil, Gas & Energy Law, 2*(3).

Stevens, P. (2016). *International oil companies: The death of the old business model*. Chatam House.

Stevens, P. (2018). *The role of oil and gas in the economic development of the global economy*. Oxford Scholarship. https://doi.org/10.1093/oso/9780198817369.003.0004

Stivachtis, Y. A. (2021). A Mediterranean Region? Regional security complex theory revisited. *Vestnik RUDN, 21*(3). https://doi.org/10.22363/2313-0660-2021-21-3-416-428

Stocker, J. (2012). No EEZ Solution: The politics of oil and gas in the Eastern Mediterranean. *The Middle East Journal*, 579–597.

Street, C. W. (2016). *OPEC Concedes Defeat in Anti-Shale Oil War with US Los Angeles: Breitbart*. http://www.breitbart.com/big-government/2015/05/28/opec-concedes-defeat-in-anti-shale-oil-war-with-u-s/

Taliotis, C., Howells, M., Bazilian, M., Rogner, H., & Welsch, M. (2014). Energy security prospects in Cyprus and Israel: A focus on natural gas. *International Journal of Sustainable Energy Planning and Management, 3*, 5–20.

Tan, K. H., & Perudin, A. (2019, April–June). The 'Geopolitical' factor in the Syrian Civil War: A corpus-based thematic analysis. *SAGE Open*, 1–15.

Taneri, I., Bilgen, G., Şahin, S., & Berument, H. (2019). *Aphrodite natural gas field and its economic viability*. [B.' Energy Notes BEN]. No028.pdf (bilkent.edu.tr).

Tastan, K., & Kutschka, T. (2019). *The implications of Eastern Mediterranean Gas for Turkey*. German Marshall Fund of the United States.

The Century Foundation. (2013). *East Mediterranean pipeline dreams*. Contributor: Allison Goodtcf.org

The Syrian Report. (2021). *Syria's Oil and Gas Industry – A sector profile*. syria-report.com

ToI. (2014). *Untangling the Turkey-KRG Energy Partnership: Looking beyond economic drivers* (p. 2). Istanbul Policy Center.

Trenin, D. (2007). Russia redefines itself and its relations with the West. *Washington Quarterly, 30*(2), 95–105.

Tsafos, N. A. (2015). *Egypt: A market for natural gas from Cyprus and Israel?* Foreign and Security Policy Paper Series.

Tsakiris, T. (2018). Importance of the Eastern Mediterranean Gas for the EU Energy Security: The role of Cyprus, Israel, and Egypt. *Cyprus Review, 30*(1), 25–50.

Tsakiris, T., Ulgen, S., & Han, A. K. (2018). *Gas development in the Eastern Mediterranean: Triger or obstacle for EU-Turkey Cooperation?* [FEUTURE Online Paper No. 22].

Tuathail, G. Ó. (1998). *The geopolitics reader: Thinking critically about geopolitics*. Routledge. ISBN 0-203-44493-0.

U.S Embassy in Athens. (2019). *Joint Declaration Between Cyprus, Greece, Israel, and the US After the 6th Trilateral Summit*. US Embassy & Consulate in Greece (usembassy.gov).

U.S. Energy Information Administration. (2012, April 12). *Global natural gas consumption doubled from 1980 to 2010*. https://www.eia.gov/todayinenergy/detail.php?id=5810#

UKOG. (2021). *Why oil is important?* https://www.ukogplc.com/page.php?pID=74

Ulusoy, K. (2008). Turkey and the EU: Democratization, civil-military relations, and the Cyprus issue. *Insight Turkey*, 51–76.

Ulusoy, K. (2020). Turkey and Israel: Changing patterns of alliances in the Eastern Mediterranean. *Journal of Balkan and Near Eastern Studies, 22*(3), 415–430.

# References

Umbach, F. (2016). The intersection of climate protection policies and energy security. In *Transatlantic energy relations* (pp. 104–117). Routledge.

UN Security Council. (2019). *Report of the Secretary-General on His Mission of Good Offices in Cyprus (S/2018/919)*. Para. 23, 2019-11-14-sg-go-report-s-2019-883.pdf (unmissions.org).

US Congress, Eastern Mediterranean Security and Energy Partnership Act. (2019). S.1102 – 116th Congress (2019–2020): Eastern Mediterranean Security and Energy Partnership Act of 2019 | Congress.gov | Library of Congress.

USNI News. (2022). *Russian Navy masses 16 warships near Syria*. Presented by "Sam LaGrone". Retrieved February 9, 2023, from https://news.usni.org/2022/02/24/russian-navy-masses-16-warships-near-syria

Wahab, B. (2023). *Tipping point of the Iraq-KRG Energy Dispute*. Emirates Policy Center. https://epc.ae/en/details/brief/tipping-point-of-the-iraq-krg-energy-dispute

Washington Kurdish Institute. (2021). *Kirkuk and Its Arabization; Historical Background and ongoing issues in the disputed territories*. www.dckurd.org

Winrow, G. M. (2016). *The European Energy Landscape*. Global Energy Debates and the Eastern Mediterranean.

Wolfrum, S. (2019). *Israel's Contradictory Gas Export Policy*. [SWP comment No. 43].

Wood Mackenzi. (2011, December). *Perspectives on Gas Exports from Israel*. www.gov.il

Woodward, P. (2016). *US Foreign Policy and the Horn of Africa*. Routledge.

Worldometer. (2016). *Syria Natural Gas*. worldometers.info

Yegin, M. (2022). United States Policy in the Eastern Mediterranean. *Comparative Southeast European Studies*, *70*(3). https://doi.org/10.1515/soeu-2022-0030

Yellinek, R. (2020, March). *Opinion – Pipelines and politics: Natural gas connects Israel and Egypt*. E-International Relations. https://www.e-ir.info/2020/03/04/opinion-pipelines-and-politics-natural-gas-connects-israel-and-egypt/

Yergin, D. (2020). *The new map: Energy, climate, and the clash of nations*. Penguin Press.

Yildiz. (2017). *The changing dynamics of Kurdish Politics in the Middle East* (p. 1). Centre for Historical Analysis and Conflict Research.

Zachariadis, T., & Hadjinicolaou, P. (2014). The effect of climate change on electricity needs – A case study from Mediterranean Europe. *Energy*, *76*, 899–910.

Zoppo, E. C. (1982). The Mediterranean in American Foreign Policy. *Revista de Estudios Internacionales*, *3*(1). Enero-marzo.